Angels, Mysteries, and Miracles

A Progressive Vision

Bruce G. Epperly

Energion Publications
Gonzalez, Florida
2017

ISBN10: 1-63199-404-2
ISBN13: 978-1-63199-404-3
Library of Congress Control Number: 2017949992

Energion Publications
P. O. Box 841
Gonzalez, FL 32560

energion.com
pubs@energion.com

With gratitude to the people
of South Congregational Church
and the pilgrims who join us for
theological and spiritual reflection each week.

TABLE OF CONTENTS

CHAPTER 1

THERE IS MORE!

Jacob left Beersheba and set out for Harran. When he reached a certain place, he stopped for the night because the sun had set. Taking one of the stones there, he put it under his head and lay down to sleep. He had a dream in which he saw a stairway resting on the earth, with its top reaching to heaven, and the angels of God were ascending and descending on it. There above it stood the LORD, and he said: "I am the LORD, the God of your father Abraham and the God of Isaac. I will give you and your descendants the land on which you are lying. Your descendants will be like the dust of the earth, and you will spread out to the west and to the east, to the north and to the south. All peoples on earth will be blessed through you and your offspring. I am with you and will watch over you wherever you go, and I will bring you back to this land. I will not leave you until I have done what I have promised you." When Jacob awoke from his sleep, he thought, "Surely the LORD is in this place, and I was not aware of it." He was afraid and said, "How awesome is this place! This is none other than the house of God; this is the gate of heaven. — Genesis 28:10-18

The story is told of fifteenth century European mapmakers who appended the western edges of their maps with the words, *Ne Plus Ultra*, "there is no more." Six centuries ago, most educated people, including church leaders, assumed that the world was flat and that ships sailing toward the far horizons would eventually fall off the planet. Despite legends describing a land beyond the seas, they believed that what they had *not* seen or experienced did not, and could not, exist. Following the voyages of Columbus and other European adventurers, these same cartographers were compelled to revise their maps with the words, *Plus Ultra,* "there is more." While they had no idea about the riches of the land and the gifts of its inhabitants, their imaginations were expanded to embrace the mysterious landscapes of this new found land.

No doubt, the same phenomenon occurred thousands of years earlier, when North America's first inhabitants revised their maps of reality in response to what they discovered on expeditions to the world beyond the Bering Straits. There is more! Reality calls us beyond our comfort zones to imagine and then venture toward new horizons of experience.

HELP IS ON THE WAY!

David discovered there was more to reality than he previously imagined when he heard a woman's voice calling to him in the middle of the night. "David, keep your eyes open, your future awaits you." A skeptic and agnostic by disposition, David initially consigned the message to the realm of dreams, or perhaps his own confusion at waking up in the middle of the night. To his surprise, the next night, he heard the same admonition conveyed by what sounded like his deceased mother's voice, "David, pay attention." While David had no idea what such a vision meant, he vowed to keep his eyes open throughout the next few days. More alert than usual, the next morning as he enjoyed his morning coffee at a local coffee shop, David found himself picking up a newspaper and no-ticing an ad for a teaching position in the local paper's advertising section. It was a synchronous moment. He had dreamed about teaching high school, but had almost given up after several unsuc-cessful interviews. Moreover, he typically never read newspapers, preferring to receive news and job openings on-line. Excited by the possibility of teaching, David sent his resume to the local school district. When he arrived for his interview, he was stunned to see a banner reading, "Your future awaits you."

Today, David is happily teaching high school English. "This may not be a big deal to some people," he admits, "but listening to that voice totally changed my life. I still don't know where it came from or whose voice it was, but now I trust my intuitions and believe that some higher power is at work in my life, pointing me toward my destiny. Perhaps, my mother's love for me was stronger than death." David discovered that there was more to life than he had previously imagined. Although he is still agnostic in many ways, David now attends a progressive Christian church, but registers his surprise that "talking about mystical experiences seems off limits in my otherwise open and intellectually curious congregation."[1]

Susan's map of reality was transformed, when her car broke down on lonely stretch of road, west of the Cape Cod village of Truro. "It was late, and I was scared. Highway 6 was deserted and snow was starting to fall and the wind was picking up. Soon conditions would make driving dangerous. Worse yet, my cell phone battery had died. A woman, all alone, late at night on a deserted stretch of road, my anxiety grew with each passing moment. It was then that I saw a burly woman, walking down the road, wearing an old army jacket and Red Sox cap. 'What's wrong?' she asked, and when I told her about my car problems, she told me to pop the hood for her to take a look. After a few minutes of fiddling with things, she called out, 'Turn on your ignition and give it a try, now!' The engine turned over, roaring back to life. A moment passed, and the hood was still up. When I went outside to investigate, no one was there. Nor could I see anyone walking along the highway." Years later, Susan still wonders, "Who was that stranger? Where did she come from? Was she my guardian angel or an anonymous Good Samaritan passing by? She had to be real. How else would

---

1   In certain cases, I have altered names and details to protect the privacy of the persons mentioned in this book.

my car have started?" In response to that mysterious encounter, Susan keeps her eyes open for persons in need, providing aid with the supplies she stockpiles in her car's trunk and routinely calling the local police when she feels it prudent not to stop. She believes she encountered an "angel unawares" (Hebrews 13:2) and now she wants to be an angel to others.

Over the past fifty years many cartographers of the Spirit have, like Susan and David, made similar exclamations, "There is more to reality than we had previously imagined. The world is more mysterious and marvelous than we had thought." While once people avoided discussing religion outside church and were reticent to share mystical and paranormal experiences for fear of being branded as eccentric or, much worse, mentally unbalanced or heretical, today millions of persons have embarked on spiritual quests and the majority of North Americans report having had mystical or psychic experiences. Paranormal visions, meaningful coincidences, angelic encounters, and near death experiences have compelled ordinary people like Susan and David to revise their maps of reality to include a mysterious and alluring spiritual realm just beneath the surface of everyday life. Most of them aren't fully sure about "what" they experienced, but they know that these mysterious visions and encounters have changed their lives, rescuing them from peril, providing spiritual guidance, and giving comfort and companionship in grief.

Still, some of these spiritual adventurers feel uncomfortable about sharing their experiences in church. As one Presbyterian woman confessed to me, "if I share my experience of an encountering an angel, they'll think I'm strange and maybe a little bit unhinged." In the words of the pastor of a liberal Protestant congregation, "I might lose my liberal credentials among my colleagues, if I told them that I saw an angel hovering over the pulpit one weekday morning. They'd think I'd gone holy roller or Pentecostal!" Their reticence to share their mystical experiences is a reminder that many mainstream and liberal Christians are "still in the closet" in terms of sharing their most life-shaping spiritual experiences.

NATURALISTIC MIRACLES

I believe that the church's calling is to be a laboratory for spirituality, healing, and mystical experiences, a place where people can feel not only safe but comfortable talking about paranormal experiences and God encounters. I believe that the spiritual realm is not necessarily supernatural or otherworldly but embedded in and continuous with our everyday lives. Reality is much more amazing and multi-dimensional than we can imagine. Like the joke about Elvis sightings, God, like the rock star, can be seen everywhere and synchronous and providential encounters can emerge in the course of daily life for those who have eyes to see and ears to hear! In fact, in a multi-dimensional universe, mystical experiences, angelic encounters, and God-sightings may be the norm for those who look more deeply into everyday life.

Today's spiritual adventurers affirm that God is not an outsider, a stranger to creation, but that the Spirit or Soul is ever-present throughout the universe, urging us and our world toward greater love, beauty, and creativity. There is more! There are burning bushes on every city street and, as Jewish wisdom proclaims, above every blade of grass an angel whispers, "Grow, grow!"

The growing recognition of a deeper spiritual realm, undergirding and permeating everyday life, has been reflected in changes in the North American spiritual landscape: the increased interest in healing within Christian as well as non-Christian communities; focus on meditative practices as pathways of self-transcendence and inner peace; studies of paranormal experiences (clairvoyance, precognition, telepathy) sponsored by major universities; and the proliferation of accounts of angelic guidance and protection. Although until recently, most liberal Christians, including ministers, discounted such experiences as vestiges of an earlier, superstitious era, or violations of strict and unbending cause and effect relations necessary for daily life, today many Christians, including a growing number of progressive Christians, are opening to a broader world view in which naturalistic miracles occur and spiritual experiences provoke radical amazement. With the emergence of quantum physics, chaos theory, complementary medicine, and scientific speculation on the origins and evolution of the universe, or multiverse, spiritual seekers have ventured beyond the limitations of materialistic, closed-system science toward a vision of reality in which mind and matter and science and spirit are intimate companions.

The scientific, medical, and religious separation of body and mind, matter and spirit, and God and the world, emergent in the sixteenth century under the influence of figures such as Isaac Newton and Rene Descartes, has given way to a more imaginative, open-ended, and holistic understanding of the universe that includes the intricate and intimate connection of spirituality and embodiment and God and the world. Once upon a time, theologians believed that God set the universe in motion and then retired to the sidelines, leaving our world totally in the thrall of mechanistic and materialistic cause and effect relationships. These deistic thinkers believed God existed as first cause, but did not participate in the day to day activities of creation-management. Most philosophers and theologians also believed that mind and body represented two virtually unrelated realms, the incorporeal and the corporeal. These dualistic and materialistic visions of reality eventually led to pushing the Spirit to the sidelines and exorcising God from everyday life. In the religious realm, spirituality focused primarily on heavenly things, the state of your soul and the hope for eternal life, and had little or nothing to say about the concrete world of health, economics, and politics. If God entered our world at all, it was believed God's entrance would be from the outside, and supernatural in character, thus violating the predictability of nature upon which we depend. Like a Saturday's parent, who appears only on special occasions to wow her or his children with parties and visits to theme parks, the image of God portrayed by deism and super-naturalism had little or nothing to do with the conduct of everyday life and the ongoing movements of the universe. Miracles and spiritual beings were discounted as anomalous and eventually unnecessary fabrications for "humanity come of age." Even mind and spirit become superfluous to many scientists, philosophers, and physicians, as the term "ghost in the machine" came to describe the absence of any inherent spirituality and creative intellectual activity in concreteness of human experience.

Yet, how things have changed in the past fifty years! While some scientists and humanists still ardently proclaim the death of God and the ethical benefits of atheism, millions of people are experiencing "something more." An increasing number of scientists are studying the sacred, especially in terms of the positive impact of spiritual practices, religious commitments, and prayer in a quantum universe. Like the European mapmakers of the 15th century, physicists and physicians have been compelled to revise their maps of reality in light of the discovery of the Higgs-Boson "God particle," whose existence has opened the door to new conversations between scientists and spiritual leaders, not to mention humorous quips such as, "The Higgs Boson walks into church. The priest says we don't allow Higgs Boson in here. The Higgs Boson says, 'But without me how can you have Mass!'" Indeed, apart from the new horizons of experience emerging from a growing partnership of science, spirituality, and mysticism, religion stagnates, becoming increasingly irrelevant to the adventures of today's spiritual pilgrims.

Today, many theologians and pastors need to catch up with the emerging interest in mysticism, religious pluralism, and holistic medicine among their congregants. Congregants have mystical experiences and near death visions, but often discover that the least hospitable place for revealing them is in the church, despite the fact that the world's great wisdom traditions had their origins in mystical, mysterious, paranormal, and miraculous experiences. Just think of mystical legacy of Judaism and Christianity: Jacob dreams of a ladder of angels and receives a blessing; Moses encounters a burning bush and discovers his life vocation; Jesus heals the sick, casts out demons and rises from the dead; Mary encounters the resurrected Jesus in the garden; and the apostle Paul has a vision of the light of Christ as he journeys toward Damascus. Though often pushed to the sidelines of institutional religion, the message of mystics such as Columba, Julian of Norwich, Hildegard of Bingen, Meister Eckhart, Ignatius of Loyola, and George Fox, have energized and reformed the church. Their experiences have inspired everyday followers of Jesus to embark on their own spiritual quests and affirm their own experiences of the Holy.

TRUSTING OUR EXPERIENCE

When I taught spirituality and medicine at Georgetown University Medical School in the 1980's and 1990's, I often reminded my students that even if you can't find a medically-documented reason for a particular symptom, you must trust your patient's experience of pain or discomfort. Doctrine, like medical data, is important in the ongoing journey of faithful persons and institutions, but just as important are our experiences of joy, wonder, celebration, and desolation. Just as significant also are mystical and paranormal experiences that push the limits of our previous understandings of God, the world, and human possibility. We may not be able to explain near death experiences, telepathy, synchronicity, mystical visions, or encounters with angels, but we need to honor these experiences and adapt our world views to make room for the possibility that they point to deeper and higher dimensions of reality, just as real, despite their mysterious nature, as our sensory experiences. We need to transform our doctrines and visions of reality to make room for such mystical and paranormal experiences, rather than fitting these experiences into outmoded and constraining understandings of religious experience and authority. These spiritual experiences should not be relegated to the Twilight Zone. They reveal elements of reality, undetectable by materialistic science or the five senses. Accordingly, they invite us to see the world, people around us, and ourselves as more awesome and wonder-full than we had previously imagined.

This text honors and affirms the mystical experiences that gave birth to the world's great religions in the context of our current and emerging scientific and medical visions. It also affirms the importance of numinous and mystical experiences of everyday people in charting the spiritual maps of the 21st century. Although we cannot always document the source of these experiences, I believe that these mystical experiences are not abnormal or supernatural, but reflect the inner movements of God's Creative Wisdom and Gentle Providence.

To some persons, who demand that God act unilaterally and coercively and solely in supernatural ways to suspend the laws of nature, my approach will appear to place limits on what God can do in our world. These theological and doctrinal "police" need an absolute God, reigning on high who comes and goes as "he" wants, violating with impunity causal relationships solely as a matter of whim. To those who hold fundamentalist religious viewpoints, and some old school liberals can be just as theologically inflexible as biblical literalists, my naturalistic approach to spirituality appears to deny divine omnipotence and places in jeopardy the uniqueness of Jesus and the faith he inspired. In contrast to these spiritually confining visions, I believe that theistic naturalism or naturalistic spirituality opens us to experiencing God in undramatic as well as dramatic ways. God is here and present in every event. Divine providence gently shapes the evolution of the universe and the growth of a child into an adult. Naturalistic theism affirms: "The realm of God is among us" (Luke 17:21 my adaptation). It also proclaims, "Cleave the wood: I am there; lift the stone and thou shalt find me there!" (Gospel of Thomas, 77). Moreover, theistic naturalism, the belief that God works within the world and not from the outside, affirms that our world is permeated by Spirit. We are constantly touched by divine providence and may even, at times, be "touched by an angel." Spirit is embodied and flesh is inspired in the God-breathed universe revealed by mystics, physicists, and people who just happen to encounter angelic beings in the course of their daily activities.

While theological wisdom challenges us to carefully examine claims of angelic encounters and paranormal, near death and mystical experiences, we also need to remember, as one philosopher noted, that philosophers err more in what they deny than in what they affirm. Following the motto of the state of Missouri, the "Show Me State," examining the evidence is always essential, but our investigations need always to be accompanied by imagination, wonder, and willingness to honor those mystical experiences that have so far eluded us.

The theme of this text, "Angels, Mysteries, and Miracles" was inspired by a conversation among members of our congregation's women's spiritual book group, who asserted "We want to learn something about angels." Initially, I was surprised. In my three years of ministry at South Church, the only time I had spoken of angels was at our Christmas Eve Service. Angels are not regularly invoked in our rationalist-oriented Congregational tradition. Still, their interest reflected changes in our congregation and in the landscape of North American mainstream Christianity and culture at large. We have a growing number of congregants who practice Tai Chi, Qigong, and yoga, read books on the intersection of spirituality and science, give Reiki healing touch treatments, and report having synchronous, mystical, and near death experiences. The emerging spiritual interest in our congregation and community led to our congregation sponsoring a class in theological reflection that inspired Energion's publishing of *From Here to Eternity: Preparing for the Next Adventure* (Energion Publications, 2016). It also led to my teaching an eight-week class on "Angels, Mysteries, and Miracles," involving twenty-five persons from our church and the wider Cape Cod community. This text emerged from lively and insightful dialogues on themes such as angelic encounters, demons and Satan, synchronicity, paranormal or psychic experiences, and the healings of Jesus that stretched our theological world views and opened us to a greater sense of God's presence in daily lives. The fruits of these conversations are found throughout this text as I sought to integrate my own theological reflection with the questions and experiences that emerged among the class members. We just scratched the surface in our eight week class, and in the open-ended spirit of the class, my goal is to present a progressive, but not all encompassing, theological vision that provides a framework for understanding where experiences of angels, demonic beings, synchronicity, paranormal experience, and physical and spiritual healing fit in our fast-paced technological and scientific world.

There is more! We are seeing the quest for "something more" in our churches today. We find new horizons of spirituality in meditation and prayer groups, healing services, and conversations about the mysterious and paranormal. I am grateful to the participants in my theological reflection seminars for their willingness to venture forth on the high seas of creative theological reflection and, in that spirit, I dedicate this text both to my Cape Cod congregation, South Congregational Church, United Church of Christ, in Centerville, Massachusetts, our community participants, some of whom traveled nearly 50 miles to come to class, and to the growing numbers of spiritual pilgrims, seeking to explore new theological and spiritual horizons in the interactions of Christianity, mysticism, pluralism, and contemporary science.

CHAPTER 2

ENTERTAINING ANGELS?

In the sixth month the angel Gabriel was sent by God to a town in Galilee called Nazareth, to a virgin engaged to a man whose name was Joseph, of the house of David. The virgin's name was Mary. And he came to her and said, "Greetings, favored one! The Lord is with you." But she was much perplexed by his words and pondered what sort of greeting this might be. The angel said to her, "Do not be afraid, Mary, for you have found favor with God. And now, you will conceive in your womb and bear a son, and you will name him Jesus. He will be great, and will be called the Son of the Most High, and the Lord God will give to him the throne of his ancestor David. He will reign over the house of Jacob forever, and of his kingdom there will be no end." Mary said to the angel, "How can this be, since I am a virgin?" The angel said to her, "The Holy Spirit will come upon you, and the power of the Most High will overshadow you; therefore the child to be born will be holy; he will be called Son of God. And now, your relative Elizabeth in her old age has also conceived a son; and this is the sixth month for her who was said to be barren. For nothing will be impossible with God." Then Mary said, "Here am I, the servant of the Lord; let it be with me according to your word." Then the angel departed from her.   – Luke 1:26-38

"Sometimes you just need an angel." That's what Paige said as we met over coffee at a Claremont, California bistro. "I was going through a deep depression and wasn't sure I was going to make it. When I looked toward the future, it was completely dark. I saw no options ahead for me except more of the same — depression and loneliness — despite my apparent success in the academic world. I attended church school as a child, but left angels and Jesus behind in college. They just weren't relevant, until…I hit bottom one weekend. Alone with no engagements or companions, I realized that I couldn't go on much longer. I loved no one and no one loved me. I cried out to the universe, not really expecting a response, 'God, help me.' Weary I went to bed, though it was only 2:00 p.m. and was rudely awakened an hour later by a knock at the door." What happened next, Paige can't explain, and she doesn't feel she needs to. The unexpected visitor came, as she now believes, as an answer to her prayer. A slightly overweight, white haired woman, acting somewhat confused, or so it seemed, related that her car had broken down a block away and she needed to use the phone. "Somehow I knew it was okay to invite her in, and so I offered her my phone, and some cool water."

As we waited for the tow truck, she told me her story, about being lost when she was my age, and then finding peace of mind by helping others. She said she wasn't very churchy, but lived by the wisdom of the scripture, 'Nothing can separate me from the love of God'" (Romans 8:39). As her guest, Nancy shared her story, and Paige began to feel a great peace descend on her. When Nancy said it was time for her to leave, Paige was sorry to see her go. Nancy concluded her visit by telling Paige how much a local church meant to her. "It's not formal or stuffy, just welcoming," she noted and left with the invitation, "Perhaps, I'll see you there sometime."

The next day, Paige chose to drop by the church Nancy attended and was sad that her new friend was not in attendance. When she asked the pastor about Nancy, she couldn't recall anyone who fit her description and stated that there was no "Nancy" on the church rolls and hadn't been for several years. To this day,

Paige admits that "I thought I was helping an older woman, who was really an angel helping me. I felt a peace, knew I could find a path forward, and later found a community of friends at the small urban church Nancy recommended. At the very least, Nancy was an answer to prayer. God provided help in the way I needed it and when I most needed it."

Was Nancy an angel, sent by God in answer to Paige's cry for help? Or, was she just a confused mother figure who dropped by out of the blue, and was able to restore Paige's spirits with her listening ear and calm counsel? "I'll never know for sure, who came to my door," Page confesses. "But, now I know that God answers prayers. I'm living proof."

A member of my "Angels, Mysteries, and Miracles" class at South Congregationl Church recalls regularly walking down a deserted stretch of road late at night on her way home from work. "It was a long time ago, so my memory has dimmed a bit. But I recall, despite the warnings that my short cut was dangerous, that I never felt afraid. I always felt God's presence walking beside me. I never saw anyone, but I knew I was not alone." The class participant recalls her shock when, a few years later, friend asked her about the identity of her companion. "Who was that tall, muscular guy who walked you home at night when you were in high school? Was that your boyfriend? I know you wouldn't have walked home alone on that road without a companion." Unknown to her at the time, my class participant really did have a companion whose presence may have frightened off potential threats. "I wonder," she admits, "if this was my guardian angel? And I wonder if this angel is still with me, guiding me and keeping me out of trouble?"

ANGELS AMONG US

It has been said that "God is like Elvis. You'll see him everywhere." The same might apply to angelic sightings in the past fifty years. As a child, I heard my parents relating a story about my grandfather, Bill Baxter, who one day "saw an angel riding a bicycle." No analysis was given, so to this day I still wonder, "Was my grandfather riding a bicycle or was the angel on a bicycle?" These days, of course, you'll find angels in the popular media as well as the religious press. In response to an overly intellectual, analytic, and technological culture, that had exorcised from the world all things mysterious and spiritual, there has been a renaissance in the intuitive, mystical, and spiritual aspects of the universe, including angels, demons, and miracles. The emergence of mystical visions in popular culture has led to humorous anecdotes as well as life-transforming testimonies. Years ago, an editor appended on a piece I wrote for the *Disciple* on "Angels in Bethlehem," a photo of a piece of jewelry, with the caption, "I'm the Archangel Michael, and I drove Satan out of heaven, and you think I'd make a nice stick pin!" An equally humorous cartoon captures two lizards in deep conversation, one of whom asserts, "I was Shirley MacLaine in a past life."

Popular angels can be superficial, but they also express our recognition that we need a Higher Power and Wisdom to navigate the challenges of our swiftly-changing, precarious, and uncertain world. In the midst of ever-emerging complexity and confusion, many of us, like the popular music group *Train,* are "calling all angels." We need, as the band cries out, a sign to know that God is here.

Angels have always been intriguing. Even if angelic portrayals stray significantly from the biblical vision of divine messengers to humankind, images of angels have captivated the public, whether in the Clarence's quirky quest for wings in the film *It's a Wonderful Life* to angelic beings who show up at pivotal moments in the television programs *Highway to Heaven* and *Touched by an Angel.* We intuitively know that there is "something more" to life than matter and consumerism, and more importantly we recognize and need a deeper wisdom and strength to turn us from darkness to light and help us find our way. The quest for angelic guidance, characteristic of our time, led me to write alternative progressive lyrics to the popular evangelical song, "We are Standing on Holy Ground," initially penned by Bill Gaither:

> We are standing on holy ground
> With countless loving angels all around
> We don't see them or hear a sound as
> Angels guide our paths toward holy ground.
> Through the ages they light our way
> Bringing help to troubled people every day
> Words of challenge and words of cheer
> God gives us holy angels now and here.

Angels remind us that we are always on holy ground. After a dream of angels ascending and descending from heaven, Jacob, the trickster and shady entrepreneur, proclaims in astonishment, "Surely the Lord was in this place and I was not aware of it" (Genesis 28:16). Jacob renames the place, "Bethel" or "Beth-El," meaning "the house of God." From his dream — and the ancients saw dreams as conveying divine messages and revealing the deeper realities of life — Jacob discovers that "Beth-El" is right where he is, but more than that, wherever he goes!

While most people don't claim to be theologians in the academic sense, everyone who asks questions of life's meaning — our origins and destiny — is a theologian. Theological reflection emerges from moments of joy and sorrow and birth and death. We are driven by these moments of ecstasy and agony to ponder whether we are alone in the universe, navigating the complexities of life and death solely by our own meager spiritual compasses, or whether there is deeper providence and wisdom that guides our days. When we cry out, calling for angels or asking for help, are we met with sheer silence or do we discover the gentle providence of God?

Given the preponderance of superficial texts on angelic guidance, often from televangelists and popular religious figures, we need to think seriously about the meaning of angelic encounters in our time. How we understand God's presence can be a matter of life and death, hope and despair, and hospitality and violence. On our way to a theology of God's presence in the world, we need first, with Hippocrates to "do no harm," and then formulate imaginative and life-giving visions of divine providence and angelic presence, grounded in scripture, experience, tradition, reason, and the best insights of our current cultural setting. Accordingly, in light of the current interest in angelic encounters, we need to begin with theological and scriptural witnesses, all the while remembering that both scripture and theology are finite and limited and point toward realities that go beyond words or explanations. In the spirit of Zen Buddhist wisdom, scripture and theology point to the moon but are not the moon — the ultimate reality — itself.

DEFINING ANGELS?

My first response to the possibility of defining angels is that "it can't be done." Angels can be experienced, not fully defined. They belong to the numinous realm, the territory just beyond our known world, and the horizon that recedes even as we venture toward it. In theology, though not necessarily economics and family budgeting, there is a virtue in vagueness. This is the point of the creative tension between the *kataphatic* and *apophatic* in theological reflection. The *kataphatic* way — "with images," in the Greek — celebrates the incarnational nature of God and God's messengers. We can experience God's presence and then talk about God and God's ways in the world, using images and words from our daily lives.

In the interplay of humility and affirmation, we discover that although we cannot fully define the angelic, we can affirm the accounts of people who report life-transforming encounters with divine messengers, who appear in their lives at the right place and right time to deliver them from danger or provide guidance for the next steps of their journey. Even if we can't determine with any certainty the source of their encounters, we have to admit that people, including hard headed realists, experience the angelic! Angels are experienced in all shapes and sizes, but almost always in a persona that enables us to hear their message or that draws us from self-preoccupation to praise.

The prophet Isaiah had just such an encounter with the divine. Isaiah describes his mystical encounter in the Jerusalem Temple:

> *In the year that King Uzziah died, I saw the Lord sitting on a throne, high and lofty; and the hem of his robe filled the temple. Seraphs were in attendance above him; each had six wings: with two they covered their faces, and with two they covered their feet, and with two they flew. And one called to another and said: "Holy, holy, holy is the LORD of hosts; the whole earth is full of his glory."*   – Isaiah 6:1-3

As I read this angelic encounter, I wonder if only Isaiah, among the throngs worshiping at the Jerusalem Temple, experienced a dramatic revelation of God's presence. Was he the only one to discover his life's vocation as prophet to a wayward nation that day in the Temple? Like the resurrection stories, most angelic encounters amaze and transform us, even as they take us into uncharted spiritual territory. It is clear that people experience the angelic and describe angels in a variety of ways — as majestic, protective, powerful, attractive, consoling, and companioning. God comes to us in ways that we can understand and angels appear often as persons like ourselves, sharing our language and ethnicity. Still, we need to remember that "there is more" to the angelic and this is the wisdom of *apophatic* or negative theology — "without images" — that reminds us that God and God's messengers can never fully described or limited by human concepts. God is here, but God is more. We must see the relativity of every doctrine and religious experience in light of the God of the universe, whose loving care encompasses billions of galaxies throughout the nearly fourteen billion year journey of our particular universe. Still, as humans, we need guideposts in our descriptions of God. Though we must hold onto them lightly, we need words and images to describe what is beyond our understanding. Speak of angels, but do so carefully, knowing that they come from a realm that neither eye has seen or ear has heard. The length and breadth of God's presence both inspires and humbles those who have been "touched by an angel."

Nevertheless, building on scripture, experience, and theological reflection, angels have been described as: spiritual beings, created by God, eternal, attentive to God's vision, caring for humanity, joining heaven and earth, and seeking the welfare of humankind and creation. Disembodied, angels appear as embodied creatures. Finite, angels deliver God's infinite wisdom. Eternal, angels share in the unfolding of time and help shape our personal and corporate histories. Fully present to God, angels see their mission as bringing humankind to an experience of God in the complex and intricately connected world of time and space. Free and creative, angels use their freedom and creativity to embody God's vision for the universe and particular human lives.

Some theologians have described "choirs" or hierarchies of angels with the most perfect of the angelic host in attendance to God and the "lower" angels assigned to share God's ways with humanity and protect vulnerable persons. While it is possible that angels, like humans differ in insight, energy, personality, and wisdom, the traditional view of hierarchies of angels reflects the three story universe — heaven above, earth in the middle, and the underworld beneath us — and the dualism of spirituality and embodiment. From the traditional hierarchical perspective, the unchanging is superior to the changing and matter is inferior to spirit. In contrast, a holistic vision of divine omnipresence and omni-activity asserts that God is fully, although uniquely, present in all places and times. God energizes our cells as well as our souls. God inspires history and human creativity, and a Living God is constantly creating — and changing — in relationship to the ongoing history of the universe. While some places are more fully incarnational than others and some persons more fully reveal God's vision than others, the world, as the philosopher Alfred North Whitehead affirms, lives by the incarnation of God. Angels who get their "hands" dirty in the messiness of human life are just as exalted as those who presumably gaze at God's grandeur and sing praises throughout eternity.

Indeed, our experiences of angelic beings reveal God's concern for the minute and often difficult details of our lives.

God's love for the world is not partial or limited to the "beautiful" and "inspiring." Just as a parent's love includes diapers, hospital visits, and tantrums as well as refrigerator drawings, learning to walk, and laughter, God's love embraces the totality of our experience, threat, conflict, and violence, as well as loyalty, love, and sacrifice. Our experience of angels gives us a glimpse into God's character as intimate and loving, and fully committed to the well-being of the least of us and the worst of us, protecting the innocent and restraining the dangerous. Encounters with angels inspire us to affirm:

> God loves us.
> God is concerned with the minute details of our lives.
> God is concerned with everyone's life,
>   not just our friends and fellow citizens.
> God communicates in a variety of ways.
> God inspires us in every encounter,
>   and sometimes we notice it!
> Help is always on the way.
> The world — and ourselves — are always more wonderful
>   than we can imagine.

ANGELS IN SCRIPTURE

The Bible describes the interplay of divine providence and human responsiveness. The Bible is moreover a library of angelic encounters and the standard by which Christians evaluate their experiences of the paranormal and the messages of angelic beings. In scripture, angels appear virtually everywhere from dreams to battlefields. Angels provide comfort, protection, guidance, and revelation. As messengers of God, biblical angels enter our lives at pivotal personal and historical moments. We can turn away from their guidance. But, for those who say "yes" to angelic messages, life becomes an adventure in companionship with God. The mun-

dane becomes miraculous and persons discover their own divinely
inspired callings.

Of the nearly two hundred fifty accounts of angelic visitations
in scripture, I will be focusing on four angelic encounters related
to Jesus' birth and resurrection. Scripture affirms that the birth of
Jesus is rooted in time and place. "In the sixth month the angel
Gabriel was sent by God to a town in Galilee called Nazareth, to a
virgin engaged to a man whose name was Joseph, of the house of
David. The virgin's name was Mary" (Luke 1:26-38). Gabriel comes
with amazing news. Mary will be the mother of God's messenger
and savior. Scripture doesn't detail the physiology of incarnation.
It simply portrays Gabriel's announcement and Mary's response.
Angels are seldom coercive and the scripture implies that Mary
could have said "no." But, the miracle of incarnation is revealed
in Mary's willingness to follow God's vision, whatever the consequences may be. "Here am I, the servant of the Lord; let it be with
me according to your word."

Gabriel comes with a message and words of reassurance. "Do
not be afraid, for you have found favor with God." Biblical angels
are seldom the cutie patootie or cherubs portrayed in art and kitsch.
They can be, as Isaiah discovered in his own angelic encounter,
terrifying in their grandeur. Mary was perplexed and amazed at Gabriel's presence and message, and needed some angelic reassurance.
We don't know what form Gabriel took in relationship to Mary,
but it was one that ultimately invited trust and confidence in God.

Mary's fiancé Joseph needed a similar dose of trust and confidence (Matthew 1:18-25). His betrothed was pregnant and he was
not the father! You can imagine his anger and suspicion. Despite
his ambivalence, he wants to do the right thing and minimize any
humiliation or punishment that might incur as a result of Mary's
unplanned pregnancy. Anxious and uncertain as to what the future
will bring Joseph decides to sleep on it. As he closed his eyes, did he
pray for God's guidance? Did he beg for divine wisdom in carrying
his plan to break off the engagement? Whether spoken or not, I am

sure that Joseph called upon a power and wisdom greater than his own. His prayers were answered with an angelic visitation.

> *An angel of the Lord appeared to him in a dream and said, "Joseph, son of David, do not be afraid to take Mary as your wife, for the child conceived in her is from the Holy Spirit. She will bear a son, and you are to name him Jesus, for he will save his people from their sins." All this took place to fulfill what had been spoken by the Lord through the prophet: "Look, the virgin shall conceive and bear a son, and they shall name him Emmanuel," which means, "God is with us." When Joseph awoke from sleep, he did as the angel of the Lord commanded him; he took her as his wife.* — Matthew 1:22-24

An angel came to Joseph in a dream. While we may discard this story because of its dream-like character, we need to remember that our spiritual parents believed that God comes to humankind in many ways, including dreams, visions, and intuitions. As Swiss psychiatrist Carl Jung asserted, dreams provide messages from the unconscious mind to provoke personal transformation or provide insight into our daily lives. An omnipresent God may give us wisdom in unexpected encounters, books we read, intuitions and hunches, and also in dreams. God moves through both the conscious and unconscious mind and is as present in the darkness as in the light. In Joseph's angelic encounter, the angel once again reassures this perplexed fiancé with the words, "do not be afraid" and then gives Joseph a life-transforming message: this child comes from God and will be God's messenger of salvation. Like his beloved Mary, Joseph says "yes." In the "yes" to God's way given by Mary and Joseph the world finds healing and wholeness.

Angels come to the least as well as the greatest. In the biblical story, the poor and powerless, and those who recognize their own sin, are often more open to divine guidance than the wealthy and self-righteous. In the nativity stories, God comes to the magi, educated and wealthy strangers from a strange land, and God also comes to shepherds, at the lowest rung of the economic ladder.

Inspiration and guidance is available to everyone, especially those who are aware of their need for divine wisdom and affirmation.

> *In that region there were shepherds living in the fields, keeping watch over their flock by night. And an angel of the Lord appeared to them, and the glory of the Lord shone around them, and they were filled with fear. And the angel said to them, "Be not afraid; for behold, I bring you good news of great joy which will come to all people; for to you is born this day in the city of David a Savior, who is the Messiah, the Lord. This will be a sign for you: you will find a child wrapped in bands of cloth and lying in a manger." And suddenly there was with the angel a multitude of the heavenly host, praising God and saying, "Glory to God in the highest heaven, and on earth peace among those whom he favors!"*

> *When the angels had left them and gone into heaven, the shepherds said to one another, "Let us go now to Bethlehem and see this thing that has taken place, which the Lord has made known to us." So they went with haste and found Mary and Joseph, and the child lying in the manger.*   – Luke 2:8-16

Once again, the visitation of angels provokes terror and awe. Angels represent the God of the universe. As C.S. Lewis says of Aslan, the Christ figure of the *Chronicles of Narnia*, "he is not safe, but he is good!" The Living God and God's messengers should provoke awe and wonder. Who are we compared to the God of 125 billion galaxies? What significance do we have in the 13.7 billion year adventure of divine creativity? At first glance, we are nothing. Yet, the One who present everywhere treasures every creature and has a vision for us in our time and place. To humble shepherds, the angels proclaim God's glory and announce that God is revealed among people like themselves, a helpless baby, the child of working people, lying in manger, birthed in a stable.

Many people have reported angelic encounters following the death of a loved one. At such moments, we are truly lost and our world has been forever changed. We need an angel, a word of reassurance that "all will be well and all will be well and all manner of thing will we well," as God spoke in a vision to the English mystic

Julian of Norwich. In the aftermath of Jesus' crucifixion, Jesus' followers' world had collapsed. They had lost their teacher, friend, and companion. His message of hope and healing for all creation had been defeated and the future was bleak. No doubt they wondered how they could go on. In such moments, angels often appear to reassure, guide, and give hope for the future.

On Easter morning an empty tomb is not enough for Mary Magdalene. Her dearest friend, the one who brought her from darkness to light, and revealed her deepest self to her, is now gone forever. She wonders if she can go on. She needs an angel and also an encounter with Jesus.

> *But Mary stood weeping outside the tomb. As she wept, she bent over to look into the tomb; and she saw two angels in white, sitting where the body of Jesus had been lying, one at the head and the other at the feet. They said to her, "Woman, why are you weeping?" She said to them, "They have taken away my Lord, and I do not know where they have laid him."* — John 20:11-13

Did these angels roll away the stone? Were they present simply to provide sufficient comfort — a spiritual and emotional transition — for Mary to take the next step? Are these angels part of Jesus' entourage? Mary is grief-stricken until she hears Jesus call her name. Now she knows that Jesus is alive and her spirit soars.

Sent by God, these angels of birth and resurrection give guidance, provide assurance, and show us our vocation as part of God's vision for humankind. Angels don't solve all our problems or answer every question. They don't coerce but present provocative possibilities and pathways to the future for us and the world. They show up in concrete situations where healing and wholeness is needed and new possibilities for humanity need to be embodied. We are free to disregard their messages, and to be overwhelmed by their presence and paralyzed in fear. Still, they call us to something more. The angels call us to incarnate God's vision in the here and now and to become messengers of God's vision ourselves. They call us to abundant life and healing in a death-filled and broken world.

GUARDIAN ANGELS

Our scriptures program that wherever we go, God is with us. In fact, nothing can separate from God's love embodied in a Gentle — and occasionally — dramatic Providence that guides our steps and shapes our encounters. Psalm 139 proclaims:

> *Where can I go from your spirit?*
> *Or where can I flee from your presence?*
> *If I ascend to heaven, you are there;*
> *if I make my bed in Sheol, you are there.*
> *If I take the wings of the morning*
> *and settle at the farthest limits of the sea,*
> *even there your hand shall lead me,*
> *and your right hand shall hold me fast.*
> *If I say, "Surely the darkness shall cover me,*
> *and the light around me become night,"*
> *even the darkness is not dark to you;*
> *the night is as bright as the day,*
> *for darkness is as light to you.*

While divine omnipresence, to some extent, renders the need for guardian angels superfluous, nevertheless both scripture and tradition affirm that spiritual beings watch over us, protect us, pray for us, and serve as intermediaries between God and ourselves. The film *It's a Wonderful Life* describes the appearance of Clarence, an angel in search of his wings, at the moment George Bailey attempts suicide. Clarence reminds Bailey that, in spite of his apparent business failure, his life has touched countless people, directly or indirectly, for the good.

Traditions within Judaism, Christianity, and Islam, describe angels being assigned to each person. After he intercedes before God on behalf of the children of Israel to prevent divine punishment for their worship of a golden calf, God promises to send an angel to go before for him as Moses leads his wayward community

(Exodus 32:34). Angels minister to Jesus as he faced temptations in the wilderness (Mark 1:9-13). Psalm 91:11 promises that, in times of conflict and trail, God will:

> *... command his angels concerning you*
> *to guard you in all your ways.*
> *On their hands they will bear you up,*
> *so that you will not dash your foot against a stone.*
>   – Psalm 91:11-12

In Jesus' introductory words to the Parable of the Lost Sheep, Jesus asserts that God is watching over the most vulnerable among us, our children: "Take care that you do not despise one of these little ones; for, I tell you, in heaven their angels continually see the face of my Father in heaven" (Matthew 18:10). Jesus' words suggest that every child of God is assigned a spiritual companion whose mission is to bridge the gulf between divinity and humanity and mediate God's wisdom to fallible and vulnerable humankind. In the spirit of the Parable of the Lost Sheep, guardian angels reveal God's intimate concern for our lives and God's deep commitment to our well-being.

Perhaps the most interesting tale of guardian angels occurs in the apocryphal Book of Tobit, written approximately two hundred years before the time of Jesus. The Book of Tobit relates the story of a pious Jew Tobit who sends his son Tobias on a journey to recover a small fortune that was owed to him. In the course of his journey, the angel Raphael joins Tobias, disguised as one of Tobit's relatives, and in the course of the journey assists Tobias in finding a wife, saves him death at the hands of a demon, and provides an elixir to restore his father's sight. This folk tale serves to remind us that God always provides for our deepest needs. In the spirit of Celtic Christianity, every place is a "thin place," in which God's vision is revealed through angelic companions or the events of our lives.

Accounts of guardian angels and angelic visitations in times of need are reminders that we are never alone and without resources.

As embodiments of God's love for us, guardian angels, seen or unseen, give us hope that in the fiery furnace or the lion's den, God will make a way where we can discern no path ahead. God is constantly delivering us from evil and temptation, even though most of the time we are unaware of it. Guardian angels witness to Paul's affirmation that "in all things God works for good" and that "if God is for us, who is against us?" (Romans 8:28, 32). Angels gives us the courage and confidence that "we are more than conquerors through him who loved us" (Romans 8:37).

In their accounts of guardian angels, persons describe experiences of deliverance and protection. They are lured from pathways ways of darkness to thoroughfares of light. Still, guardian angels are neither coercive nor omnipotent. They present provocative possibilities for us to consider and shape in our own unique way. Moreover their impact on our lives is part of an intricate spiritual ecology, which includes our past history, current personal situation, quality of spiritual life, and the influence of external events. According to tradition and experience, guardian angels, as manifestations of God's love, will not abandon us even when we walk through the darkest valley, the valley of the shadow of death.

A THEOLOGY OF ANGELS

As a matter of full disclosure, I must confess that have never consciously encountered an angel. However, it is clear to me that we cannot limit the scope of reality to what we have or have not (yet) experienced. When I taught religion and medicine at Georgetown University's School of Medicine, I regularly reminded my medical students that they should trust their patients' perceptions of pain, even if they could not be objectively verified through medical tests. I counseled my medical students, "If the patient says she has pain, she has pain, and it's your task to honor her experience." The same counsel applies to our reflections on the existence and impact of angelic messengers. Like near death experiences, synchronous encounters, or life-changing intuitions, encounters with angels transform peoples' lives, often bringing hope in times of despair, courage in times of fear, and guidance in times of confusion. Although no external observer may be able to verify them, these dramatic experiences carry their own spiritual validation for those who have angelic encounters.

Experiences of angelic protection suggest that there are forces in the universe, more highly evolved than humankind, that are unabashedly on our side and that a Gentle, and sometimes Fierce, Providence guides our lives in a variety of ways. When Isaiah has a vision of seraphim in the Jerusalem Temple, he hears these angelic messengers proclaim the foundational truth of mystical experience, "Holy, Holy, Holy is the Lord of Hosts; the whole earth is full of his glory!"

Angels announce that the whole earth is full of God's glory. God's glory — the sheer wonder of divine creative wisdom and love — is revealed to a teenage girl, soon to be the mother of the healer and savior of humankind, to a troubled fiancé, to shepherds in the fields, a grieving friend, and to a future prophet struggling to find his way in a time of national crisis. God's glory is revealed to the shifty entrepreneur Jacob in terms of a ladder to heaven, with angels ascending and descending. Jacob exclaims, "How awesome is this place! This is none other than the house of God, and this is the gate of heaven" (Genesis 28:17). Jacob's dream tells us that every inch of our planet is the house of God and, for those who awaken their senses, every place can become the gateway to heaven. God's angels are earthly as well heavenly minded. They may, as the Book of Tobit witnesses, be as concerned with domestic issues of marriage, economics, and health. Spirituality concerns the whole of life, and not just our eternal destiny.

God's glory is everywhere. In all things, God seeks our well-being. God is revealed in the smallest and largest of events, in the darkness as well as the light. Still, if God is omnipresent, what purpose do angels have in God's relationship with the world? Do we really need angels in a God-filled world? Can't we just assume angels are divinity in disguise and that rather than looking for angels, we shouldn't we be looking for God? All these are good questions, and they help us reframe our understanding of angels in terms of a holistic, interdependent universe, in which God is here in us and among us and not confined to a faraway celestial realm.

In an interdependent universe, far different in nature than the three story universe our spiritual parents imagined, God doesn't need intermediaries. Still, in a holistic universe in which body, mind, and spirit, and heaven and earth, interpenetrate one another, angelic companions have an important role as revelations of divine wisdom and protection. Divine representatives enable us to experience God's vision in ways we can understand. No one can fully experience God. God's grandeur is beyond what any word or doctrine can relate. That is the wisdom of the *apophatic* way. Yet, God is also embodied and understood in terms of our day to day lives. That is the complementary wisdom of the *kataphatic* way, which affirms that the indescribable God is also our intimate companion.

No one can fully fathom God or angelic beings, nor can we dismiss the impact of deceased saints or life-companions on our day to day lives, especially to those who include beloved friends and exemplary religious teachers in their prayers. Nevertheless, I believe that God can manifest God's wisdom and love in terms of tangible messengers and companions, whose primary reality is spiritual, and who are not bound by the limitations of our wonderful, yet messy, space-time world. Perhaps, there is a deeper naturalism, in which non-local causation, spiritual immediacy, clairvoyance, and travel through time and space in the blink of an eye is the norm. We catch a glimpse of the spiritual interdependence of life in rare moments, described as mystical, psychic, synchronous, or precognitive in nature. Our only occasional mystical experiences may be the norm among certain spiritual beings, such as divine messengers. The appearance of angels, accordingly, is miraculous in revealing the deepest life-changing energies of the universe, but it is not supernatural. Angelic messengers do not disrupt the predictable cause and effect structure of the universe. They reveal the all-pervasive intentions of the Wisdom and Energy that gives birth to the universe and sustains each moment of our lives.

God is not "out there." God doesn't need to be manipulated into our lives through prayer nor does God have to supernaturally bridge the chasm between heaven and earth or spirit and matter. God is here, fully here. That is the meaning of divine omnipresence and omni-activity. Angels remind us in tangible ways that "heaven" is already here; we just aren't aware of it!

In their encounters with humankind, angels embody divine possibilities. They push us beyond the known to the unknown. They reveal to us that "there is more" to life than our limited perspective and ambiguous past behaviors. They also remind us that we are not the "crown of creation" and that reality is much more wonderful and multi-dimensional than we can imagine. Poet Walt Whitman once proclaimed, "All is miracle." The utterly miraculous nature of everyday life is the testimony of angelic messengers, whether they announce "Glory to God in the highest" to awestruck shepherds or tell equally awestruck followers of Jesus that Jesus is not in the tomb, for he has risen.

Over two decades ago I appeared as a "theological expert" on a cable news program devoted to encounters with angels. After hearing the other guests describe marvelous, life-changing and life-saving encounters with angels, the host turned to me and asked a question way above my theological or spiritual paygrade, "When something goes wrong, does that mean that your guardian angel was asleep or off duty?" After taking a deep breath, I realized that she was asking a deeper question, "In a God-inspired world, why do we suffer? Why do bad things happen to us, if angels are watching out for us?"

No one can fully fathom the problem of evil or suffering or how much power God or angels have to protect us. If angels — or God — as benevolent and loving in character could prevent meaningless suffering, I am sure they would. But, as I've written elsewhere, freedom and creativity are at the heart of reality.[1] While God and God's messengers seek healing and wholeness in every situation, they have to contend with and work within causal processes that involve creature-like choice and creativity, social influences, and the energies of the natural world. Neither God nor God's messengers are coercive or all-determining. In fact, I believe that God, like the best of parents, encourages maximal freedom and creativity congruent with the well-being of the whole. God influences all things, but does not determine all things. Even microscopic realities such as rapidly proliferating cancer cells can appear to defeat God's aim at abundant life. Angels may provide comfort to the dying and give dying persons glimpses of everlasting life, but they may not be able to change the course of an incurable illness.

With no warning, terrorists attack a night club in Orlando, Florida, and an airport in Istanbul. Surely their actions do not reflect God's will or God's work. Yet, God and God's messengers must live with the pain and grief felt by their survivors. More than that, God feels their pain and sense of loss. Perhaps, angels were watching over Pulse in Orlando or a Bible Study at Emmanuel African Methodist Episcopal Church in Charleston, South Carolina. Their presence was surely sympathetic and intimate, and their angelic pain was real. Yet, even the guardian angels could not stand between a bullet and its intended victim, nor could they turn the killer away from his intent to destroy God's beloved children.

God is the fellow sufferer who understands and the fellow celebrant who rejoices. God is gently moving our world toward the good in each moment, but God — like us — must live with pain, failure, and uncertainty. Beyond their hymns of praise, angels may also lead us in lament, keeping our hearts open to pain when we are tempted to spiritually and emotionally shut down. God's messengers, whether in terms of angels or our own deepest feelings — what Abraham Lincoln called our "better angels" —

---

1   Bruce Epperly, *Process Theology: Embracing Adventure with God* (Gonzales, FL: Energion Publications, 2014) and *Process Theology: A Guide for the Perplexed* (London: Continuum, 2011).

calls us to become God's companions in healing the world and choosing courage and compassion rather than fear and hate. In the words of Mr. Rogers, following the 9/11 terrorist attacks, in times of trouble, "When I was a boy and would see scary things on the news, my mother would say to me, 'Look for the helpers. You will always find people who are helping.'" Amid tragedy, angels may manifest themselves working alongside us, bringing healing to our communities, and inspiring us to make a way when there is no way and providing us with a "second wind" to face apparently insurmountable challenges. Look for the helpers. They may be angels in disguise.

I believe that although God is present everywhere, some moments and encounters more fully reflect God's presence than others. These incarnational encounters and moments reflect the interplay of God's vision and human openness. Like us, God can choose to be more present in some situations than others. God was deeply present in Jesus, and Jesus as "fully alive" embodied the glory of God for us and our salvation. God is everywhere and in all things — "cleave the wood and I am there," as the Gospel of Thomas exclaims. God is the reality "in whom we live and move and have our being," (Acts 17:28) as Paul philosophizes. Yet, we need "a God with skin," and that's the meaning of Jesus' incarnation, fully representative of God's vision, in our messy, intricate, wonderful flesh and blood world. Although angels, as spiritual beings, don't exactly have "skin," they appear in embodied ways, influencing our lives in tangible and life-changing ways, helping us start cars, frightening would-be assailants, and appearing to a teenage girl with marvelous tidings of salvation. Angels witness to the faith, embodied in words from "A New Creed" from the United Church of Canada:

We are not alone,
we live in God's world....

In life, in death, in life beyond death,
God is with us.
We are not alone.

Thanks be to God.

Spiritual Practice: Calling on Angels

Awakening to the Angelic

Recently, many congregations have debated about whether to eliminate the "Invocation" at the beginning their worship services, preferring to use the language of "Call to Worship" or "Call to Awareness." To many contemporary Christians, God is already here and doesn't need to be "invoked." The use of invocations suggests a world in which a distant God, who would otherwise ignore us, comes to us as a result of our prayers. In truth, God doesn't need to be "invoked," but we do. The ever-present God is constantly providing guidance, intuition, and protection, but most of the time we are unaware of it. Moreover, God's call precedes our response. Though our prayers of invocation and awareness reflect our desire to experience God's presence, our prayers are inspired by the Gentle Providence that is as near as our next breath.

In the biblical tradition, God's angelic messengers come as God's initiative and not our own. They reflect God's deepest desires for us, and not our ego's need for gratification, success, power, or prosperity. More often than not, encountering an angel is initially overwhelming. Angelic beings often comfort persons with the words, "Don't be afraid," despite the fact that angels reveal themselves in ways we can experience and, on occasion, understand.

Our scriptures assert that we are at God's beck and call, and not the other way around. We are called by God through inspiration, insight, challenge, and companionship. Our cries for help reflect the Spirit speaking within us "in sighs too deep for words." When we call upon God, we open ourselves to a Wisdom and Power that is already present and waiting to respond to our deepest needs.

Today, many people want to contact their angels and spirit guides. A spiritual marketplace, populated by spirit channels and workshop leaders has emerged to help people contact their guardian angels. Small fortunes are spent at workshops intended to awaken us to our angelic companions. There is nothing inherently wrong with this practice, provided its goal is aligning with God's vision and desire for us rather than seeking to align God's will to our desires. Even when persons come to God imperfectly, motivated by their own self-interest — and that is all of us — God still wishes us experience the deepest desires of our hearts, ultimately found in relationship with the One to Whom All Hearts are Open and All Desires Known. While some spiritual teachers have complicated and multi-step processes to access divine wisdom, it is my belief that the wisdom of God is already here, available to us at any moment. In our quest to encounter God's angelic messengers, we may discover that God has already provided the guidance and inspiration we need.[1] God is a Loving Parent, who gives us "more than all we can ask or imagine" (Ephesians 3:20). Still, as Jesus promises, our openness to God shapes God's presence and power in our lives:

> *Ask, and it will be given you; search, and you will find; knock, and the door will be opened for you. For everyone who asks receives, and everyone who searches finds, and for everyone who knocks, the door will be opened.* – Matthew 7:7-8

---

1 Representative of many approaches to contacting spirit guides or guardian angels, Asandra, author of *Ask Your Spirit Guides* (Schiffer, 2011) presents a fourteen step process including preparing the environment, breathing and centering , asking for protection, chanting, going through a mental doorway, inviting your guardian angels to contact you, asking for a sign, and giving thanks. (http://www.beliefnet.com/wellness/2010/09/contact-your-spirit-guides.aspx?)

Sometimes the simplest prayers are the most effective. While I am strong adherent of meditative prayer and spend nearly an hour each day in prayerful contemplation or centering prayer, I also believe that simple prayers awaken us to the divine guidance we need, whether it comes to us in the form of angelic messengers, insights and inspirations, dreams, intuitions, bursts of healing energy, or synchronous encounters. The following simple prayers have been helpful in awakening to God's ever-present wisdom and protection:

- "Help!"
- "Lord, have mercy upon me, a sinner."
- "Show me the way."
- "Guide my steps."
- "Show me the path to take and the words to speak."
- "Awaken me to your Loving Presence."
- "Lead me, guide me."
- "Let me do your will, O God."

Awakening to God's presence is as simple as the prayer from the Compline or Evening Prayer Service of the Episcopalian/Anglican *Book of Common Prayer:* "O God, make speed to save us. O Lord, make haste to help us." Recognizing that God is our source of salvation transforms us from lonely isolation to graceful interdependence, and opens us to the energy of grace residing in every moment of experience.

When we put God at the center of our prayers, we will receive the deepest desires of our hearts and the wisdom we need to respond to life's challenges. Like Mary and Joseph, saying "yes" to God's vision may involve sacrifice and suffering. We may need to simplify our lives and winnow what's unnecessary. We may even need to let go of certainty and security, trusting that God will guide our steps. Whatever lies ahead, we can trust the angelic words, "Fear not, for God is with you," for "nothing can separate us from the love of God in Christ Jesus our Lord" (Romans 8:39). So, call upon the angels in times of need, knowing that as you call for God's messengers, you are calling for their Master and that God will send you what you need to experience healing and wholeness, whether directly through an insight, through a "chance" encounter, or through an angelic or human companion.

CHAPTER 3

THE DEVIL, YOU SAY?

In those days Jesus came from Nazareth of Galilee and was baptized by John in the Jordan. And just as he was coming up out of the water, he saw the heavens torn apart and the Spirit descending like a dove on him. And a voice came from heaven, "You are my Son, the Beloved; with you I am well pleased." And the Spirit immediately drove him out into the wilderness. He was in the wilderness forty days, tempted by Satan; and he was with the wild beasts; and the angels waited on him. – Mark 1:9-13

During my twenty year tenure as a university chaplain and professor at Georgetown University in Washington DC, I often climbed the famed "Exorcist Steps" on my walks to and from the university and Georgetown. During the daytime, running up the steps provide a great aerobic workout. But at night, the wary pilgrim might experience — mostly in her or his imagination — the presence of malign forces and decide to give the steps a wide berth, choosing a more secular pathway home.

Humans have always been both afraid of and attracted to the shadow side of life. In the light of day, we feel in control; the rational mind is at work building and planning and creating worlds in which we are masters of our fate and captains of our destiny. But, come nighttime, the shadows and things that go bump in the night remind us that we are always just a moment away from entering the Twilight Zone or have passed beyond the Outer Limits. We realize that beneath the surface of what we can understand and control, there is another world — the realm of the unconscious, the spirit world, where dreams, ghosts, angels, and demons inhabit. Even if such worlds are more reflective of our psyches than external and tangible spiritual realities, they remind us that there is universe beyond our sunlight machinations and that we may become the victims of dark and subterranean forces that shape our day to day lives; malign forces that may, at times, come to possess people and institutions. The uncanny descriptions of demonic forces and spirit possession remind us that there are times when our personal or communal well-being may require the intervention of benevolent powers greater than ourselves.

Just as the angelic has become the subject of popular media, the demonic has also become the theme of movies and television programs, ranging from *The Exorcist* and *Rosemary's Baby* to *Ghost Hunters* and *Ghostbusters*. The attraction of such films is not only their eeriness and the need for a good scare every so often, but the deep recognition, mostly tamped down by the conscious mind, that we are never fully in control of our lives. When we do something out of character or inadvertently commit a social faux pas, we may exclaim, "What possessed me to do that?" Or, "That wasn't me!" We may be stunned by observing riots emerging at soccer games, cult groups committing mass suicide, serial killings, or whole countries falling under the control of malevolent and narcissistic leaders. We can't imagine that we as twenty-first century humans are capable of such irrationality and destructiveness, and yet history shows otherwise. Moreover, we hear reports of cases of ritual abuse, religious groups traumatizing their members, especially young children. We have heard of persons who seem to be controlled by multiple personalities, each with its own dietary needs, allergies, vocal patterns, and emotional characteristics and intellectual capabilities.

While most cases of dissociative identity or multiple personality disorders can be attributed to survival mechanisms emerging to protect persons psychologically during times of childhood trauma and abuse, there are occurrences in which malignant forces appear to be at work, taking over human personalities and forcing them to do their bidding. While we may laugh at Flip Wilson's signature line, "the devil made me do it," we may nevertheless wonder whether or not demonic forces are at work in the world, revealing themselves in the actions of hate groups, brutal killings, political parties run amuck, and the inability of rational people to make life and death decisions regarding issues of hunger, economics, and global climate change. We wonder: Are there spirits of violence, greed, or apathy? Is there a reality hell-bent on challenging God's aim at Shalom, abundant life for all creation?

Throughout history, religious traditions have affirmed the presence of benevolent spirits — angels, divas, and spiritual guides — who bring healing, salvation, and enlightenment to the human race. Religious traditions have also described malign forces, tempting us to choose evil and self-interest rather than goodness and care for well-being of the community. While no religious tradition has fully explained the presence of such evil forces in a universe supportive of our deepest spiritual aspirations, our faith traditions have recognized the existence of evil spirits, internal or external to the human psyche, whose impact is most fully revealed in the incorrigible reality of sin, separation, violence, and ignorance.

While many images of the demonic are humorous — caricatures of red men with horns carrying pitchforks - these images point to a deeper reality. A reality either housed in the human psyche or in realities beyond ourselves; the existence of a dark side, evils that rise from within, and powers that take over the rational mind, destroying our own willpower and making us subservient to their whims.

In the context of the winsome and positive visions of spirit guides and channeled entities described by "new age" spiritual teachers, there is another contrasting vision of the spirit world. This vision projects a dark counter-force to beings of light, a malevolence that contests against the benevolence of angels, spirit guides, saints, and family members interceding on our behalf from the spiritual realm. Evolution does not guarantee goodness among more evolved creatures. Lack of a body does not always insure wisdom or kindness. In human life, intelligence is, on occasion, mated with brutality and sadism. Power is often joined with manipulation and destruction. While we cannot fully describe these dark forces, and may come to believe that they are primarily emotional and unconscious in nature or revelatory of the spirits of groups and institutions, the reality of sin and evil will not go away and points to spiritual counter-forces operative in a God-filled and God-loved universe. The historic "problem of evil" finds its expression not only in human sin, incurable illness, and natural disasters, but in the stories we tell — the myths and legends — of Satan and the demonic forces that support Satan's cause.

WHAT THE DEVIL! THE DEMONIC IN SCRIPTURE

The Biblical accounts of Satan and his minions are challenging and confusing, to say the least. Over the centuries, Satan appears to have evolved from the role of district attorney, or "devil's advocate" within the divine court, taking on the task of evaluating Job's piety, to becoming God's evil antagonist and the leader of the spiritual forces of darkness.

The Hebraic scriptures, or Old Testament, provide only modest descriptions of Satan. The wily and nefarious snake, responsible for tempting Adam and Eve to eat the fruit of The Tree of Good and Evil in disobedience of God's admonitions, is only indirectly identified with Satan, and this in retrospect, and primarily in the early Christian tradition and the later development of the doctrine of "original sin." Further, given the slow evolutionary movement toward human maturity, the mythical story of Adam and Eve may be as much about the ambiguities of growing up as descriptive of the human condition in general and not a particular historical couple. After succumbing to temptation, the legendary Adam and Eve are driven out of paradise. Mortality, conflict, and toil result from turning away from God's directive. Yet, even though they are banished from the Garden and now experience spiritual and moral ambivalence, they are given the chance to begin again. The world they "create" is ambiguous and death-filled. It is also adventurous, artistic, animate, and activist. Not unlike the experience of every child, Adam and Eve go from a state of dreaming innocence to the complexity of adulthood and responsibility. Something is lost, the immediacy of relationship with God and our families of origin, and the pure sense of living in the now. Something is gained amid the anxieties of maturity, the ability to shape the historical and cultural adventure in all its complexity, wonder, and tragic beauty.

Genesis also contains a curious story about the "sons of God" having intimate relations with the daughters of earth, producing an offspring of giants, Nephilim. This story which describes spiritual beings captivated by their lust for womankind most likely serves to explain the reason why some persons tower over their neighbors in height (Genesis 6:1-4). The "demons" described throughout the Old Testament are most likely idols or the gods of the Canaanite earth-based religions, and do not resemble certain New Testament demons, spiritual beings who may possess a person's spirit or cause physical illness. In this author's estimation, the banishing of the Canaanite gods was itself ambiguous. In the quest for divine purity, the followers of Yawheh, the sky God of Israel, eventually lost their sense of embodied wonder, and in the Christian tradition, often forsook earth and its beauty to focus on a heavenly reward. The results of a heaven-oriented religion, sadly have led to the disenchantment and destruction of our planet.

The New Testament has a richer and more complicated and problematic understanding of the demonic and Satan, the Prince of Darkness than the Hebraic scriptures. While the New Testament does not present a fully articulated theology of the demonic, the following paragraphs shed light on the early Christian movement's understanding of the malicious presence of demons in human life.

The quest for greatness is fraught with great temptation. In the late nineteenth century, Lord Acton observed: "Power tends to corrupt, and absolute power corrupts absolutely. Great men are almost always bad men." While there are many exceptions to Ac-

ton's assertion, spiritual, political, and economic power has a way
of stunting our idealism. An idealistic senator comes to Washington
DC, determined to transform our nation by restoring accountabil-
ity, promoting equality, and establishing transparency. Soon this
same senator is tempted to maintain the status quo and go along
with his or her party's leadership in order to remain in office and
gain political power. Religious leaders transform hearts and minds.
Their words are charismatic and their touch healing, but too often,
they are led astray by affluence and the adulation of women and
men. Some religious leaders reside in multi-million dollar homes
in gated communities, supported by the donations of economical-
ly-struggling followers, and sadly use their charisma to manipulate
their "worshipers" politically, financially, and sexually. Energy, power, and charisma can heal and they can also harm. Power and wealth
can be used to create, but they also can be vehicles of destruction.

Fresh from his baptism and the descent of the Spirit, Jesus
goes into the wilderness for a spiritual retreat. He has heard God's
affirmation, "you are my beloved child," and has felt divine power
surging through him. Filled with God's Spirit, Jesus knows that
he can change the world for the good. He can speak for God and
reveal God in ways that heal the sick, welcome the outcast, and
transform the sinner. Yet, Jesus wants to ground his power in spiritual maturity and wisdom.

In solitude we often discover many conflicting voices, some of
which will divert us from our true vocations. Jesus was no excep-
tion. In the wilderness, he encountered Satan. He heard the voice
of temptation coming from deep in his psyche. He may even have
encountered external forces of evil, tempting him to turn away
from God's vision, projected in the form of his diabolical opponent,
Satan (Matthew 4:1-11; Mark 1:12-13; Luke 4:1-13).

The Synoptic Gospels (Matthew, Mark, and Luke) portray
the tempter, or devil, as subtle in his temptations. He offers Jesus
food, security, and power to do good, each of which is essential to
human survival and flourishing. The problem is that succumbing
to these temptations will lead Jesus away from his mission as God's

Beloved Child and Savior. Jesus banishes Satan by placing his ultimate trust in God rather than Satan's penultimate offerings. Our greatest temptation is to believe that we have no temptation and to mistake good things for the One Good Thing that gives meaning to life, security, creativity, and power.

Mark and Luke describe angels providing Jesus nurture in the wake of Satan's departure. Adding a realistic tone, characteristic of our own struggles with temptation, Luke notes that "when the devil had finished every test, he departed from him until an opportune time" (Luke 4:13). None of us, not even God's Beloved Child can escape temptation. Our only hope is to call upon God's protection and power when we are assailed by inner or outer temptations. We don't need to believe in an external demonic power to recognize our need for grace and power in times of trial and temptation.

First century Jewish religion often identified sickness with the activity of demons, or spiritual beings loyal to Satan. Similar to today's germ theory, it was believed that illness resulted from the activities of Satan's minions, or unclean spirits, whose purposes included undermining a persons' relationship to God and diminishing their quality of physical and spiritual lives. Early in Jesus' ministry, the Healer was invited to Peter's home for supper. Alas, Peter's mother-in-law, the alpha female of the household could not feed them, due to a debilitating fever. Recognizing the importance of hospitality as part of the senior woman's responsibility, Jesus reached out to her: "He stood over her and rebuked the fever, and it left her. Immediately she got up and began to serve them" (Luke 4:30). Jesus verbally denounced and evicted the fever, the spirit of illness, suggesting that he and his followers believed that physical illness may have a demonic cause. Jesus provides a simple "exorcism," casting out the feverish demon with healing words. The passage concludes with the following statement:

> *As the sun was setting, all those who had any who were sick*
> *with various kinds of diseases brought them to him; and he laid*
> *his hands on each of them and cured them. Demons also came*
> *out of many, shouting, "You are the Son of God!" But he rebuked*

them and would not allow them to speak, because they knew that
he was the Messiah.   — Luke 4:40-41

The healing of Peter's mother-in-law and Jesus' ongoing response to demon-caused diseases reveals Jesus' power over the
demonic forces that diminish human life; that these forces recognize Jesus as their spiritual adversary; and that demonic forces can
be exorcised or sent away by God-inspired word and touch.

In the wake of *The Exorcist* and other media portrayals of demon possession, Jesus' encounter with a man possessed by demons
provides wisdom for persons involved in healing ministries. As we
explore the meaning of the man possessed by multiple demons, first
of all, it is important to remember that no one can fully fathom
or define what is perceived to be a demon, whether in this healing
story or the contemporary world. Many forms of multiple personality, or dissociative identity disorder, are the result of childhood
trauma, especially repeated physical, sexual, or emotional abuse,
in which the fragile central self becomes fragmented as a matter of
self-protection. According to the Mayo Clinic, dissociative identity
disorder can be described as follows:

> This disorder, formerly known as multiple personality
> disorder, is characterized by "switching" to alternate identities.
> You may feel the presence of one or more other people talking
> or living inside your head, and you may feel as though you're
> possessed by other identities. Each of these identities may have
> a unique name, personal history and characteristics, including
> obvious differences in voice, gender, mannerisms and even
> such physical qualities as the need for eyeglasses. There also
> are differences in how familiar each identity is with the others.
> People with dissociative identity disorder typically also have
> dissociative amnesia and often have dissociative fugue.[1]

Without a centered self, persons with dissociative identity disorders often are at the mercy of a variety of fragmented selves, each
vying for control. Studies have indicated that the various selves have

---

1   http://www.mayoclinic.org/diseases-conditions/dissociative-disorders/
    basics/symptoms/con-20031012

different voices, intellectual aptitudes, and allergies. While prayer is always indicated in any health condition, the best treatment is a secure environment, the presence of persons who serve as spiritual crucibles or holding places, counseling, and medication. The same would apply to today's epilepsy, often seen as spirit possession or a sacred disease in the first century, but hardly the result of external demonic forces.

Still, there are occasions in which persons experience themselves controlled by malevolent powers greater than themselves, which undermine their central personality. While we cannot be precise as to the source of such experiences, we must be open to the possibility influences of spiritual beings, hell-bent on our personal destruction. This appears to be the case in the story of the man possessed by a legion of evil spirits (Mark 5:1-15).

> *They came to the other side of the sea, to the country of the Gerasenes. And when he had stepped out of the boat, immediately a man out of the tombs with an unclean spirit met him. He lived among the tombs; and no one could restrain him anymore, even with a chain; for he had often been restrained with shackles and chains, but the chains he wrenched apart, and the shackles he broke in pieces; and no one had the strength to subdue him. Night and day among the tombs and on the mountains he was always howling and bruising himself with stones. When he saw Jesus from a distance, he ran and bowed down before him; and he shouted at the top of his voice, "What have you to do with me, Jesus, Son of the Most High God? I adjure you by God, do not torment me." For he had said to him, "Come out of the man, you unclean spirit!" Then Jesus asked him, "What is your name?" He replied, "My name is Legion; for we are many." He begged him earnestly not to send them out of the country. Now there on the hillside a great herd of swine was feeding; and the unclean spirits begged him, "Send us into the swine; let us enter them." So he gave them permission. And the unclean spirits came out and entered the swine; and the herd, numbering about two thousand, rushed down the steep bank into the sea, and were drowned in the sea. The swineherds ran off and told it in the city and in the country. Then people came to see*

what it was that had happened. They came to Jesus and saw the
demoniac sitting there, clothed and in his right mind, the very
man who had had the legion; and they were afraid.

Whether this story is intended to be parabolic or literal in
nature, it is not accidental that it follows Mark's account of Jesus'
calming of the storm at sea (Mark 4:35-41). Jesus' words "peace
be still" apply to natural, spiritual, internal, and external storms.
In this story, the man in question is plagued by a "legion," that is,
as many as 1500 demons, similar in number to a legion of Roman
soldiers that render him harmful to himself and others. John Dom-
inic Crossan, among others, sees his mental upheaval as the result
of chaotic powers unleashed by the Roman occupation of Judea.
At the very least, the trauma of Roman occupation may have set in
motion forces that made this man susceptible to malign influences.
Following the trauma of 9/11, many persons in the Washington,
DC and New York metropolitan areas found themselves reliving the
anxieties associated with previous traumatic experiences. Whatever
the cause, this man has lost everything, including his self. According to Mark, only Jesus can save him. Only Jesus' benevolent spirit
as God's Beloved Child can overcome the powers of darkness.

Jesus' encounter with the possessed man is a window into the
biblical world of malign spirits. First of all, the spirits know Jesus.
Often, as the gospel stories note, the powers of darkness are more
aware of God's presence and power than the children of light. Jesus
represents a threat to the status quo of malignant possession, and
the fearful spirits begin to bargain with Jesus. Jesus listens to the
demons and grants their wish. Could it be that there is an "original
wholeness," even in the demonic, that is open to divine healing? Or,
are the demons irretrievably lost? For those who affirm the power
and love of God, no creature, even Satan, is beyond salvation.
Could God be constantly asking the malign forces to come home
to grace? Could God be waiting for these forces to use the freedom
that caused them to fall from grace to eventually return to the love
that gave them life?

Jesus gives these "unclean spirits" what they want. They are released at their request into 2000 swine, who charge into the sea and are drowned. The forces of evil have to go somewhere. They don't simply disappear. The story ends with the formerly demon possessed man, "clothed and in his right mind."

This story reminds us that demonic powers are not to be underestimated. By whatever name we call it, these powers can undermine our spiritual, physical, and emotional well-being. Accordingly, I strongly caution against using games such as the Ouija board, drawing pentagrams, or calling upon Satan even for recreational purposes. I urge you to stay away from any situation involving Satanic rituals or Satanic cults, even out of curiosity. There is real evil in our world! When we venture into the spirit world, we never know what we are getting into. Although there are angelic powers and positive spiritual beings, including deceased loved ones that medical intuitives or psychics and family members appear to contact, it is best to steer clear of anything that you believe to be spiritually ambiguous or demonic. Persons may pray for anyone in need, but exorcisms and other encounters with beings presumed to be demonic, is best left to those who are specifically called and trained in such ministries. Calling on the loving name of Jesus and God's angelic messengers, embodying God's pure and unambiguous care for us, is the only safe spiritual reality in which to place your trust.

The final story of demonic influence I want to discuss is Paul's account of a thorn in the flesh. According to the apostle:

> It is necessary to boast; nothing is to be gained by it, but I will go on to visions and revelations of the Lord. I know a person in Christ who fourteen years ago was caught up to the third heaven—whether in the body or out of the body I do not know; God knows. And I know that such a person—whether in the body or out of the body I do not know; God knows— was caught up into Paradise and heard things that are not to be told, that no mortal is permitted to repeat. On behalf of such a one I will boast, but on my own behalf I will not boast, except of my weaknesses. But

if I wish to boast, I will not be a fool, for I will be speaking the truth. But I refrain from it, so that no one may think better of me than what is seen in me or heard from me, even considering the exceptional character of the revelations. Therefore, to keep me from being too elated, a thorn was given me in the flesh, a messenger of Satan to torment me, to keep me from being too elated. Three times I appealed to the Lord about this, that it would leave me, but he said to me, "My grace is sufficient for you, for power is made perfect in weakness." So, I will boast all the more gladly of my weaknesses, so that the power of Christ may dwell in me. Therefore I am content with weaknesses, insults, hardships, persecutions, and calamities for the sake of Christ; for whenever I am weak, then I am strong.   – 2 Corinthians 12:1-9

In this autobiographical account, Paul implies that Satan's messenger is unintentionally doing God's work by keeping Paul humble. Paul could be boastful and arrogant in light of his mystical experiences. But this unnamed "thorn in the flesh" serves to remind Paul that any power and wisdom he has comes from God. Like all humans, Paul is a sinner saved by grace alone. The reality of temptation and finitude, not to mention sin and mortality, drives us to trust God and God alone for our salvation. As Paul proclaims, God has told him "My grace is sufficient for you, for power is made perfect in weakness." Moreover, when we trust God to supply us with our deepest needs for inspiration, guidance, power and protection, we discover "whenever I am weak, then I am strong."

In this passage, God works within Paul's experience of the demonic to achieve God's saving purposes. In Romans 8:29, Paul affirms that "in all things God works for God for those who love God, who are called according to his purpose." Satan may intend to harm Paul by deterring him from his mission through illnesses of body or spirit, but God's Gentle and sometimes Fierce Providence transforms Satan's wiles into a blessing. Joseph's words to the brothers who betrayed him express God's providential care, revealed in the most challenging of life's situations, including the impact of the demonic: "Even though you intended to do harm to me, God intended it for good" (Genesis 50:20).

The Biblical tradition is clear that the universe is populated with spiritual beings more highly evolved than ourselves in terms of power and intellect. It is equally clear that disembodiment does not guarantee goodness. The demonic represents that which inspires humankind to choose death rather than life. The Biblical tradition is also clear that, left to our own devices, we are no match either for the temptations or emotional, spiritual, and physical machinations of these powers of evil, whether operative in our personal or institutional lives. Yet, the Biblical tradition is equally clear that Satan and his minions is no match for Jesus as the manifestation of God's healing power. In the archaic but powerful language of Martin Luther's *A Mighty Fortress is our God*, we can be open to the possibility that demonic beings exist without seeing ourselves as powerless in relationship to them. God is on our side and, at the name of Jesus, the demonic flees.

A mighty fortress is our God, a bulwark never failing;
Our helper He, amid the flood of mortal ills prevailing:
For still our ancient foe doth seek to work us woe;
His craft and power are great, and, armed with cruel hate,
On earth is not his equal.

Did we in our own strength confide,
　　our striving would be losing;
Were not the right Man on our side,
　　the Man of God's own choosing:
Dost ask who that may be? Christ Jesus, it is He;
Lord Sabaoth, His Name, from age to age the same,
And He must win the battle.

And though this world, with devils filled,
　　should threaten to undo us,
We will not fear, for God hath willed
　　His truth to triumph through us:
The Prince of Darkness grim, we tremble not for him;

His rage we can endure, for lo, his doom is sure,
One little word shall fell him.

That word above all earthly powers,
    no thanks to them, abideth;
The Spirit and the gifts are ours
    through Him Who with us sideth:
Let goods and kindred go, this mortal life also;
The body they may kill: God's truth abideth still,
His kingdom is forever.

Satan will come and go. He is a creature, like us, and his existence and influence is finite not ultimately a result of his own power. The powers of evil emerge, albeit unwanted, from the Loving Energy that gives life to and sustains all things, who contests against Satan and who will eventually disarm or transform Satan. God's kingdom is forever!

SATAN: A THEOLOGICAL EXPERIMENT

At times, in the course of writing this chapter, I wondered out loud, "Why am I writing about angels and demons? I don't know of any other progressives offering classes or writing in this area. I'm not a Pentecostal. Although mystically inclined, I am a rationalist and a hard-sell on the paranormal and spirit world. I know there is evil in the world, but I'm not sure I believe there is a personal Satan." Still, as a theologian and pastor, I must pay attention to social and cultural trends and the experiences of persons who have shared stories of spirit possession and demonic forces. Perhaps, because "I am from Missouri," (the Show Me state) theologically and spiritually, and am trying to explore territory usually off-limits in progressive theology, I am called to take this journey. I want to make sense of what may always be beyond my understanding and dialogue with those who ardently believe in the existence and power of malevolent spirits.

Every theologian or preacher who speaks or writes about the mysteries of God must always, in her or his own mind, confess "I may be completely wrong about this." Theological reflection is, by definition, limited, imperfect, and prone to false certainty. Failure to see the falsehood in our own affirmations leads to intolerance, exclusion, heresy hunting, and persecution. It also leads to claiming ultimate truth for finite and imperfect statements. The greatest idols in history emerge from having too much certainty about our doctrinal truths. Such idolatry led to the Inquisition, witch hunts, excommunication, and the violence of Muslim and Christian extremists. The devil we see in others may be the manifestation of our own fear and uncertainty.

Nowhere do we need to be more humble about our theological reflections than in our attempts to understand the reality of Satan. Too much certainty about Satan has led to persons projecting their own temptations on others, thus, scapegoating people described as heretics, pagans, and witches, as the cause of their own trials and tribulations. Doctrines about Satan as well as the anti-Christ of the Book of Revelation have also led to dividing the world into the children of light and the children of darkness, and the assumption that we are the children of light and our foes demons in disguise. This has sadly been an undercurrent in the disastrous marriage of conservative religion and politics in the United States, as evidenced in one presidential candidate calling his opponent "the devil." We have often overestimated the evil of our opponents and underestimated our own spiritual and institutional sin.

The existence and character of Satan is shrouded in myth and mystery. The reality of a diabolical force, contending equally toe to toe with God for human allegiance is unfathomable in a God-created universe. Yet, despite its moral and metaphysical implausibility, at first glance, we can talk about entropic, egoistic, malevolent forces that vie for the souls of humans and institutions.

Although I believe that theological reflection is primarily a matter of heart-felt affirmations that have the power to change our lives, our reflections on Satan must begin with negations, highlighting "what Satan is not," the first of which involves the very existence and character of Satan. Many scholars believe that the full-bodied and personified image of Satan emerged as a result of Jewish and Christian encounters with Zoroastrianism, a Persian religion whose central vision involved the eternal battle between the primordial forces of Good and Evil. According to followers of Zoroaster, these two forces will contend with one another throughout the historical adventure until the end of history, when Good triumphs over Evil. Many Christians act as if this fight to the death is true of the Christian world view as well. But, there is one significant difference that makes all the difference in the world for our spiritual and ethical lives. Satan is *not* God's equal. God is the ultimate creative force in the universe and God's creative wisdom sustains all things and every moment of our lives, including Satan and Satan's minions, as finite creatures in a dynamic, multi-dimensional, constantly creative universe. The universe could not exist for one millisecond apart from God's creative and wise energy, and that means Satan and his minions as well as us. While Luther's poetry may be accurate in its description of Satan's apparent power over us, "on earth is not his equal," this is not true of the universe as a whole. Even on earth, the "prince of darkness" is not in control, nor can Satan ever be in control if God is, in fact, omnipresent and omni-active as the Power of Love in the universe.

Satan is described as a fallen angel, but he is still an angel and that means that he is created, finite, limited in knowledge and vision, and utterly dependent on powers other than himself for his existence. If we take the biblical myths of the fallen angels seriously, even if not literally, Satan's power is less than that of the archangel Michael, whose forces defeat him in the primordial struggle between good and evil. In the visionary myth of Revelation, Michael and his angels are still at work in the world inviting us to abundant life, inspiring the church, and delivering us from evil, despite Satan's diabolical plans.

The deepest mystery of any theological exploration of the demonic is "how did Satan come to be?" What forces or proclivities made Satan God's adversary? The mythical language of Revelation 12:7-9 portrays a battle in heaven at the beginning of time:

> *And war broke out in heaven; Michael and his angels fought against the dragon. The dragon and his angels fought back, but they were defeated, and there was no longer any place for them in heaven. The great dragon was thrown down, that ancient serpent, who is called the Devil and Satan, the deceiver of the whole world—he was thrown down to the earth, and his angels were thrown down with him.*

Homeless, Satan and his angels found temporary respite in our world. Eventually, they will be banished to eternal punishment in the underworld, where Satan's kingdom awaits, according, to many Christian teachers, all who turn away from God.

In many ways, like the story of Adam and Eve, the Revelation account of Satan's fall is more confusing than helpful in understanding the problem of evil or the existence of an evil angel, Satan. Still, from this myth, emerging from John's mystical vision on the Isle of Patmos, we can discover certain important truths about the forces of evil.

First, Satan is defeated! If Satan has any power at all, it is limited and confined by God's power. Even on earth, God's power is strong and faithful, keeping Satan in check at every turn. Yes, Satan may have "victories" but they are finite and temporary and often involve our succumbing to temptation and hatred. Second, Satan as the supreme force of evil is not alone in diabolical intent; he has followers who share his vision. Third, humans are not completely at the mercy of the demonic: there are forces constantly at work to challenge Satan's intentions and these angelic forces, emissaries from the Holy One, have greater power and wisdom than Satan and his minions. Fourth, in light of the prowess of Michael and his angels, not to mention the God of the universe, we can depend on resources beyond ourselves as we confront the evils in ourselves and in the world. Satan cannot and will not win, for nothing in all creation can separate us from the love of God.

This passage also raises some serious theological challenges. First of all, what was the source of this conflict in heaven? To be honest, no one knows, although preachers and theologians have been speculating for over 2000 years. Did Satan want to usurp God's power by staging a palace coup in the courts of heaven? Did Satan envy God's love for humankind, as some rabbinical tales aver? Moreover, how could a being so intimate with God ever imagine abandoning his (or her) creator? Is God an "underachiever," to recall a Woody Allen joke, who can't even control the divine household and who lacks the ability to inspire fidelity among those most intimate with God? Is Satan — along with his followers — totally evil or is there some good in him, similar to the diabolical figure of Darth Vader in the Star Wars mythical saga? All of these questions are unanswered and perhaps unanswerable by scripture and subsequent Christian tradition.

The point of a myth is to present a vision of reality, a deeper truth of life, and not necessarily facts. Theological myths, like the best fiction, transform our lives by the insights they contain even if they were never fully embodied on earth or heaven. At the very least, the images of a battle in heaven and a counterforce to God's vision reflect the insight that there are forces — energies or personal beings — in our lives and in the universe that apparently possess a power greater than our own and that have the cunning, allure, and power to sway persons and institutions away from their highest good. This may have been true in Judas' betrayal of Jesus. It may also be evident in the bloodlust still perpetrated by religions, terrorist cells, and governments.

Still, the battle in heaven is perplexing, to say the least. As I read this mythical account, nested in the mystical and mythical vision of John on the Isle of Patmos, one important thing stands out. Agency and initiative are present at every level of the universe, from the highest to the lowest. Angels and presumably the rest of creation, including ourselves, possess freedom and creativity, and this freedom and creativity can be used for good or evil, healing or destroying. God's power is relational and works within the inherent freedom of creation. Although God will outlast any manifestations of evil, thus giving us hope for a final resolution of our and the world's wayward imperfection, we are endowed with freedom and creativity that shapes — yes shapes! — God's presence and action in the world. God must contend with the diabolical actions of ISIL/ISIS and lone wolf terrorists, the animosity from homegrown racists and bigots, and the destructive power on microscopic cancer cells, all of which appear to win the day. None of these forces, our faith tells us, will eventually defeat God's aim at love, justice, and beauty. Conversely, Satan's impact and presence in the world is shaped by, and limited by, our prayers, acts of kindness, commitment to justice, and desire to forsake self-interest in favor of world loyalty.

Theologian Walter Wink presented a vision of Satan that contrasted with the literalistic interpretations of conservative theologians and preachers. For Wink, Satan represents the "spirit" of institutions that can turn them away from their intended vocations. "Powers and principalities" exist as the deeper unconscious forces of destruction, alienation, and evil, reflective of institutional and communal values. We can see such powers in the rise of Hitler in culturally sophisticated Germany, in business institutions for whom greed cancels out any care for the common good, in riots at soccer games, in racism that "rears its ugly head" (I am using these words intentionally) both among the populace and in the halls of Congress following the election of Barack Obama as President of the United States, in congregations that fire their pastors one after another over decades, and in the spirits that seem to possess us in the form of destructive addictions, whether to drugs, alcohol, and pornography, as well as socially acceptable addictions such as workaholic behaviors, consumerism, or focus on success to the detriment of relationships.

For Wink, the demonic is not a literal person, Satan, but a living and energetic emotional-spiritual reality that emerges from dysfunctional and destructive social values and behaviors. The powers and principalities are reflected in the behavior of otherwise decent people who succumb to life-destroying influences in their communal lives. Such persons may become emotionally, spiritually, or institutionally possessed by negative powers greater than themselves. Still, in Wink's vision, there is hope for healing of these destructive powers, based in the following affirmations:

1) The powers and principalities are good. (In the myths of scripture, Satan is an angel, who falls, but he is an angel!)

2) The powers are fallen. (Emotionally, vocationally, and institutionally, they turn away from their intended purpose in God's vision of creative interdependence and Shalom.)

3) The powers can be redeemed. (God has the final word in our lives and history. God is able to repair the separation created by impact of demonic forces. God is able to heal the world. Part of the healing involves our recognition of the realities that "possess" us and our institutions and, then, prayerfully confronting and exorcising these powers.)[1]

Whether we look at Satan and the demonic from the point of view of myth, a spiritual or institutional projection, or as the reflection of actual malevolent beings, it is clear that we cannot underestimate the powers of evil to destroy what we love best. These powers of evil seem to attack persons and institutions when they are most vulnerable. In times of fear, they tempt us with security at the cost of freedom. In times of change, they tempt us with images of stability that will come to pass only strangers and infidels are banished. In times of contention, these powers and principalities tempt us with false absoluteness and the projection of evil upon those with whom we disagree theologically or politically. As powerful as these forces can be in destroying human community and turning us away from the vision of Shalom, we must remember that they are perversions of the good, and have no ultimate cosmic power to

---

1   For more on Walter Wink's understanding of the powers and principalities, see *The Powers that Be: Theology for a New Millennium* (New York: Doubleday, 1999).

defeat God's vision. In the essential freedom and creativity of the universe, evil powers can shape our lives; but so can the forces of healing and wholeness, and reconciliation and grace. Each moment gives us the opportunity to listen to the deeper voices of life, to awaken to our "better angels," God's Gentle Providence undergirding and influencing each moment of experience.

The impact of sin, poor decision-making, institutional evil, economic injustice, racism and sexism, can be great and can traumatize as well as distort God's aim at goodness, but God's "still, small voice" whispers, "You can be healed. Have faith. I am with you. You can turn around and become a new creation. Evil will not have the final word." Perhaps, Satan and his minions will eventually hear God's whisper, and like Darth Vader, choose life and love over evil and alienation. Perhaps, God will be "all in all," redeeming the world by love rather than destruction.

Spiritual Practice: Calling on Jesus

Nearly five hundred years ago, Martin Luther asserted that our only hope when Satan's power and temptation assails us to call upon Jesus and cling to his amazing grace embodied in our baptism, the community of faith, and God's word and wisdom in scripture and in our lives. In times of deep despair, Luther is reputed to have scribbled on his desk "I was baptized, I was baptized," as a reminder that his sins, papal opposition, and Satanic temptation are powerless to wrest him from God's eternal love. For Luther, baptism was a reminder that not even death or the devil can separate us from the love of God.

The biblical tradition promises that followers of Jesus have the power to triumph over Satan and his minions. After equipping his followers spiritually and theologically, Jesus sent seventy followers on a ministry of teaching and healing. Their only tools as Jesus' emissaries were prayer and faith in God. According to Luke's Gospel, "The seventy returned with joy, saying, 'Lord, in your name even the demons submit to us!' He said to them, 'I watched Satan fall from heaven like a flash of lightning'" (Luke 10:17-18).

Satan has fallen! Still, regardless of our beliefs about the nature or existence of the demonic, all of us need protection from temptation and the negative impact of our environment. Some people believe we contend against external spiritual forces of evil, such as Satan. Others see these forces in terms of the lures of materialism, sexism, racism, xenophobia, and homophobia. In either event, these powers can destroy body, mind, and spirit, and tempt institutions and nations to turn away from their true callings. We cannot ultimately be defeated by these forces because we have the grace of God and our own prayers of protection and power to respond to malevolent forces in our lives and society.

ENCIRCLED IN DIVINE PROTECTION

The Celtic Christian tradition has a long tradition of prayers of protection. Often they are joined with an encircling prayer. The "caim" or "encircling" involves rotating in a clockwise fashion while drawing a circle around yourself with your index finger and praying for God's care to surround you. As we circle ourselves, we affirm that God is with us and encircles us every step of the way. The best-known prayer of protection is the Prayer of St. Patrick:

> I arise today
> Through the strength of heaven;
> Light of the sun,
> Splendor of fire,
> Speed of lightning,
> Swiftness of the wind,
> Depth of the sea,
> Stability of the earth,
> Firmness of the rock.
> I arise today
> Through God's strength to pilot me;

God's might to uphold me,
God's wisdom to guide me,
God's eye to look before me,
God's ear to hear me,
God's word to speak for me,
God's hand to guard me,
God's way to lie before me,
God's shield to protect me,
God's hosts to save me
Afar and anear,
Alone or in a mulitude.
Christ shield me today
Against wounding
Christ with me, Christ before me, Christ behind me,
Christ in me, Christ beneath me, Christ above me,
Christ on my right, Christ on my left,
Christ when I lie down, Christ when I sit down,
Christ in the heart of everyone who thinks of me,
Christ in the mouth of everyone who speaks of me,
Christ in the eye that sees me,
Christ in the ear that hears me.
I arise today
Through the mighty strength
Of the Lord of creation.

Christ is with me in every situation and wherever my footsteps may take me. Written in a time of personal crisis, this prayer places our lives in God's protection. You may want to use a simple affirmation to sum up the protective spirit of this prayer as you draw a circle around yourself physically or in your imagination:

- God's hand guards me.
- God's wisdom guides me.
- God's love surrounds me.
- Christ is my companion.

GOD'S ARMOR OF LOVE

In light of his own temptations and his encounter with the diabolical forces threatening the existence of the early Christian movement, the Apostle Paul counseled his followers to put on the whole armor of God and clothe themselves in an armor of light. These spiritual affirmations or talismans were intended to strengthen our spirits when we face subtle and dramatic temptations:

> *Finally, be strong in the Lord and in the strength of his power. Put on the whole armor of God, so that you may be able to stand against the wiles of the devil. For our struggle is not against enemies of blood and flesh, but against the rulers, against the authorities, against the cosmic powers of this present darkness, against the spiritual forces of evil in the heavenly places.* – Ephesians 6:10-12

After reading Ephesians 6:10-12, take time to visualize God surrounding you with a protective shield. Recognize that God's protective power is greater than any external spiritual force you may face or inner temptation that may seek to lure you away from God's vision. Even when we fail to be our best, God will restore us by God's grace. Greater is God within us, than the demonic forces of the world!

Salvation and health, as Paul and the author of Psalm 23 recognized, come as we walk through the darkest valley with God as our guide and companion. We can't go around life's trials and temptations, but we can go through them knowing that God is with us and nothing can separate us from the love of God.

> *Besides this, you know what time it is, how it is now the moment for you to wake from sleep. For salvation is nearer to us now than when we became believers; the night is far gone, the day is near. Let us then lay aside the works of darkness and put on the armor of light.* – Romans 13:11-12

In times of temptation and struggle, imagine a strong and peaceful light surrounding you. This divine circle of light guides your path, illumines the evils in your way, and protects you from inner and outer threat.

THE POWER OF PRAYER

While I do not encourage laypeople to participate in exorcisms, we can pray for others' protection. We may lift up the following prayer for those who are struggling to be faithful to God in the midst of conflict, addiction, temptation, and threat:

> God of light of love, I draw a circle of protection and healing around _____. May he (or she) experience God's power and guidance. Banish all malign forces and temptations. In the powerful name of Jesus, let life, love, and light abound. Amen.

An abundance of words is not necessary in our prayers for protection for us or others. We might simply pray:

- Lord, have mercy. Christ, have mercy.
- Help me, Jesus!
- Help her (or him)!
- Make haste to save your servant.
- Deliver me from temptation. I rest in your glory.

HEALING THE SOULS OF INSTITUTIONS

Biblical spirituality claims that institutions as well as persons can be influenced by negative as well as positive spiritual forces. Walter Wink has identified the Biblical power and principalities with the emotional and spiritual energies that appear to take over nations, congregations, and communities. Polarization, mob rule, bloodlust, xenophobia and genocide, can take over institutions. Such characterizations invite us to consider questions such as: Whether a malevolent spirit possessed the German people during the Nazi regime? Is a demonic force, projected as hatred of the West, guiding ISIS/ISIL? Were decent churchgoing people possessed by the spirit of racism that inspired the cross burnings of the Ku Klux Klan and Jim Crow laws? Do we see a spirit of fear motivating USA citizens when shouting invectives and threaten refugees fleeing political and religious persecution?

In an interdependent universe, God is present as the source of creative transformation in every moment of experience. This same interdependence allows malevolent forces to influence individuals and institutions. In either case, we still have the freedom to say "yes" or "no" to God or the demonic. We can align ourselves with our "better angels" and bring forth beauty in our world. We can also turn from the good and beautiful to pursue pathways of violence, hatred, and greed.

Influenced by Walter Wink, George McClain has provided spiritual practices to cleanse institutions and their members. For example, McClain notes that following the Ku Klux Klan rally in Fort Wayne, Indiana, one hundred Christians gathered the next day to repudiate violence and racism and to reclaim the space for God. Holy water was sprinkled to reclaim the courthouse as holy ground.[1]

McClain has written a number of prayers of social and political exorcism. He believes that, without polarizing, we can awaken to and challenge the spirits that can control businesses, corporations, churches, and governments. He believes in giving prayers for guidance and protection at every meeting.[2] These prayers include:

- Prayers in advance for the meeting.
- Prayers for the space in which the meeting is held and the persons who will be present.
- Opening devotional readings and prayers to give us greater perspective and free us from powers of division.
- A person appointed to be intercessor throughout the meeting.

If conflict emerges, take time to pause, breathe deeply, and ask for God's guidance.

McClain counsels that we should pray for deliverance and renewal of conflict-ridden institutions. In the name of Jesus, we

---

1   George McClain, *Claiming All Things for God: Prayer, Discernment, and Ritual for Social Change* (Abingdon Press: Nashville, 1998),15.
2   Ibid., 78-79.

can break the power of emotional and spiritual histories that bring chaos and destruction to institutions.

> We discern that there are influences and spirits not of God which are preying upon (name of institution) and holding it captive to alien powers and principalities…..In the name of Jesus we bind these spirits and powers not of God so they can do no more evil

> ….In Christ…

> we declare that these spirits are disclosed, discredited, and stripped of their power….

> Spirit of (whatever emotion has been at work, such as fear, hatred, greed), we order you to depart from (name of institution) and surrender before God.

> God we thank you for your power over spirits which defy you. We order them to depart from (the institution) and surrender before God.[1]

However we understand these forces of evil operating in the world, we can trust that God is with us and that God's Loving Providence will overcome and outlast any malevolent realities we face. Thanks be to God!

---

1 Ibid., 129-130.

CHAPTER FOUR
ONE STEP BEYOND

Then Herod secretly called for the wise men and learned from them the exact time when the star had appeared. Then he sent them to Bethlehem, saying, "Go and search diligently for the child; and when you have found him, bring me word so that I may also go and pay him homage." When they had heard the king, they set out; and there, ahead of them, went the star that they had seen at its rising, until it stopped over the place where the child was. When they saw that the star had stopped, they were overwhelmed with joy. On entering the house, they saw the child with Mary his mother; and they knelt down and paid him homage. Then, opening their treasure chests, they offered him gifts of gold, frankincense, and myrrh. And having been warned in a dream not to return to Herod, they left for their own country by another road.
— Matthew 2:7-12

I call it the "providential butt call." One morning as I was taking a walk on the beach, I heard the sound of my phone making a call and then someone picking up the phone. "Who is it?" the voice on the other end asked. Just as I was trying to hang up, I looked at the number and recognized it as a congregant's home phone. I picked the phone up and said, "This is Pastor Bruce. I hadn't intended to call you. I'm sorry for calling you this early. My phone just dialed you up." My congregant responded, "Pastor, I'm so glad you called. My wife and I are feeling depressed today." We proceeded to talk for fifteen minutes as I walked along the seashore. As I hung up, he thanked me and said, "I'm glad God wanted you to call me, even if you weren't planning to." In response, I took a moment to pray with him, asking God to bless him and his wife and give them God's peace and healing touch. I felt grateful, too, for this unexpected "butt call." It was truly providential. I had planned to call later that morning, but I recognized that a Deeper Wisdom was at work in what appeared to be an accident. Could there have been a Gentle Providence at work in cyberspace that morning, helping me be a pastor "for just such a time as this?"

Deeper than the conscious mind, there is a Grace of Interdependence that joins us in one spiritual family. In moments of surprising grace, we discover that we are all connected and that we are — yes, all of us — constantly receiving guidance from God and that this guidance comes in the form of apparently chance encounters, dreams, visionary experiences, near death experiences, and moments in which we catch glimpses of the future and experience the deeper emotions of friends and loved ones. Every so often we wake up to this Gentle Providence and exclaim with Jacob, "Surely the Lord was in this place, and I was not aware of it" (Genesis 28:16).

In this chapter, we will take a look at those God moments, those unexpected "mysteries" which often miraculously transform our lives. While we can be open to God's Higher Wisdom, it often comes unexpectedly, awakening us to the ties that bind all of us in God's Gentle Providence. These experiences may not be supernatural violations of the laws of nature, but they have a miraculous quality as new insights, energies, and information pour into our lives from an Intelligence and Wisdom greater than our own.

In the following, we will consider the spiritual and psychic "more" that surrounds and shapes our lives. While we may not be able to say with complete authority the source of such experiences of intimate spiritual connection and wisdom, we must honor experiences that transform persons' lives. Reality, as Martin Buber is reputed to have asserted, is not always understandable, but it is embraceable. In embracing the deep mysteries of life, we may encounter Divine Wisdom and Energy for healing, wholeness, and guidance.

SURPRISES OF SYNCHRONICITY

How often have you thought of someone and then almost immediately received a phone call? Or, have wondered how a friend, with whom you haven't communicated lately, is doing and then run into her or him on the street? Or, had someone say to you, "I'm so glad you called. I really needed somebody to talk with!"

Sometimes we are in the right place at the right time. Tom had an intuition he should stay home rather than meet friends at the beach for a cookout. He really wanted to get together with his friends for a good time after a long week as a building contractor. But, as Tom says, "something inside me told me to stay put." So he went out on the porch, fired up the grill, put on a steak, and opened a bottle of beer. A few minutes later his phone rang, and his neighbor was frantically calling for help. Her eighty year old husband had just collapsed and was unresponsive. Tom dropped everything, jumped the fence, and administered CPR until the paramedics came. Tom now believes that "I was there for a reason. God planted a thought, and I paid attention, and saved a life." What is more synchronous is that Tom had just taken training in CPR with the local Red Cross.

Susan usually took a day and a half to drive the five hundred miles from her Cape Cod village to the Washington DC suburbs where her sister lived. But, this time as she hit the Philadelphia suburbs where she normally stopped to spend the night, she had a second wind. "Something," she recalls in retrospect, "was drawing me forward and giving me energy for the final leg of the trip. I felt desperate to see my sister." She arrived in the late afternoon. An hour after her arrival, Susan's sister received a call reporting that her son had been killed in an auto accident. Today, Susan says that "It was God-thing. I usually don't have the energy to make the trip in one day, but this time I did. I just had to get there by suppertime.

I didn't know why at the time. Now, I think God was drawing me toward my sister's house, so that I could be there to comfort her when she got the news. God gave me a nudge and the energy to make the trip."

The phenomenon of synchronicity is often the doorway to openness to mystical experiences, including healing and paranormal experiences. Moments of "meaningful coincidence," to use the language of C.G. Jung, remind us that there is a deeper movement in the universe, a Gentle Providence that is at work beneath the level of consciousness. In speaking of synchronicity, Jean Shinoda Bolen asserts:

> For those who have felt the power of events, dreams, and meanings that seem to contain meanings deeper than themselves, it can be a window on a world larger and more whole than the world of logical reasoning and concrete facts.[1]

According to Bolen, Jung describes three kinds of synchronicity: a coincidence between mental content (which could be a thought or feeling) and outer event; a dream or vision, which coincides with an event that is taking place at a distance (and later verified); and an image (dream, vision, or premonition) about something that will happen in the future that does occur.[2]

All of these phenomena, including synchronous events and encounters, depend on a "connecting link," described by Jung as the collective unconscious.[3] Jung's vision of a deeper reality, aimed at personal wholeness and spiritual maturity, beneath everyday conscious experiences, suggests, first, that consciousness is the tip the iceberg and not the totality of the experience. It also suggests that we have experiences that involve emotion, intuition, bodily inheritance, and empathy with others' experiences that lies beneath the conscious mind. The dynamic interdependence of the universe testifies to the fact that we can be influenced by realities faraway

---

1   Jean Shinoda Bolen, *The Tao of Psychology: Synchronicity and the Self* (New York: Harper One, 2004), xiii.
2   Ibid., 16.
3   Ibid, 36.

away from our current location and, in the case of the power of prayer, we can positively influence persons at a distance. Whether we call it Gentle Providence, the grace of interdependence, or the collective unconscious, we are part of an intricate and dynamic fabric of relatedness that is constantly moving in our lives, aiming us toward healing and wholeness.

Synchronous experiences can be life-changing but they are not necessarily supernatural. In a world in which everything is connected and divine providence is universal, we can discover moment by moment and encounter by encounter our calling "for just such a time as this." We can encounter divine wisdom, dynamic yet universal or archetypal in nature that guides our steps to fulfill our calling as God's companions in healing the world. Synchronous encounters point beyond themselves to a lively spiritual vision involving, as Jean Shinoda Bolen asserts, "the unity and interrelationship of all phenomena and the intrinsically dynamic nature of the universe."[1]

LIFE-TRANSFORMING DREAMS

Long before the emergence of Jungian psychology, the Biblical tradition described God speaking to humankind through dreams and visions that foretell the future, provide protection, and guide us toward the future. The most well-known dreams involve Jacob and the ladder of angels, Joseph the son of Jacob and advisor to the Egyptian Pharaoh, Joseph the father of Jesus, and the Magi from the East. Today, people still receive dreams and deep dream-like intuitions that provide profound personal wisdom as well as warnings about danger to themselves or others.

Let me share a story from my own family. During the early years of their marriage, my mother-in-law was a buyer for a major Cleveland, Ohio department store. Her work involved regular travel to New York City to see the latest fashions. On the eve of one of her buying trips, her husband had a deep dream-like intuition that

---

1   Ibid., 5.

she would be in danger if she took the plane home and advised her to take the train, rather than a plane, back to Cleveland. Despite having plans to take the plane back with the sales team, she chose to follow my father-in-law's advice and boarded a train home. When she arrived back in Cleveland, her husband greeted her with the tragic news that the plane had crashed, killing all her co-workers. No one could explain the source of her husband's life-saving premonition, but my mother-in-law was forever grateful that she took his intuition seriously. Had she not listened to my father-in-law's dream, my wife would never have been born.

Two thousand years earlier, the baby Jesus and his family were saved by similar protective dreams. The scriptures make clear that Divine Wisdom provides glimpses into future possibilities that we should take to heart. This Wisdom does not determine the future in its entirety but invites us to be God's companions in creating a positive future for us and those who depend upon us.

> *And having been warned in a dream not to return to Herod, they [the magi] left for their own country by another road. Now after they had left, an angel of the Lord appeared to Joseph in a dream and said, "Get up, take the child and his mother, and flee to Egypt, and remain there until I tell you; for Herod is about to search for the child, to destroy him." Then Joseph got up, took the child and his mother by night, and went to Egypt, and remained there until the death of Herod. This was to fulfill what had been spoken by the Lord through the prophet, "Out of Egypt I have called my son."*   – Matthew 2:12-15

These life-saving dreams have the quality of premonitions, visions or intuitions that give a sense of what the future may bring unless we change our course. These dreams and intuitive experiences present provocative future scenarios around which we may decide the future course of our lives. Dreams are one way that God directs us toward safety in the immediate future and over the long haul. God's vision of personal and global healing involved the safety of child Jesus. To that end, God was at work in the deeper unconscious of the magi and Joseph to insure the child's well-being.

In all things God is working for good, including the unconscious realm of dreams and intuitions.

Jacob's dream of a ladder of angels inspired him to look at his life from a new perspective, going beyond his self-interested entrepreneurial focus to recognizing his role in God's vision of history.

> *Jacob left Beer-sheba and went toward Haran. He came to a certain place and stayed there for the night, because the sun had set. Taking one of the stones of the place, he put it under his head and lay down in that place. And he dreamed that there was a ladder set up on the earth, the top of it reaching to heaven; and the angels of God were ascending and descending on it. And the LORD stood beside him and said, "I am the LORD, the God of Abraham your father and the God of Isaac; the land on which you lie I will give to you and to your offspring; and your offspring shall be like the dust of the earth, and you shall spread abroad to the west and to the east and to the north and to the south; and all the families of the earth shall be blessed in you and in your offspring. Know that I am with you and will keep you wherever you go, and will bring you back to this land; for I will not leave you until I have done what I have promised you." Then Jacob woke from his sleep and said, "Surely the LORD is in this place—and I did not know it!" And he was afraid, and said, "How awesome is this place! This is none other than the house of God, and this is the gate of heaven."*
>
> – Genesis 28:10-17

As a result of his dream, Jacob discovered that, despite his past shady business dealings, he stood on holy ground. He renamed the site of his dream, Beth-El, the gateway or house of God. He also received a larger vision of his own vocation and place in history. Although Jacob always remained somewhat ethically ambiguous, his dream awakened him to God's constant presence, protection, and guidance. While not nearly as dramatic as Jacob's dreams, many of us have dreams that reveal a deeper wisdom about ourselves, help us solve personal and relational problems, provide insights regarding our physical, emotional, and spiritual healing, or give us assurance that all will be well for us and those we love. God's wisdom comes in images and archetypes from the unconscious, midwifed by God and God's messengers for our healing and wholeness.

A few decades later, Jacob's son Joseph became a dreamer himself. He dreamed about future possibilities and then became the interpreter of Pharaoh's dream. There is a synchronicity between those who dream and those who listen to dreams. In the interdependence of life, it takes a community to interpret our dreams. Pharaoh dreamed of hard times ahead, but needed Joseph's intuitive vision to provide context and meaning. In listening to another's wisdom, Pharaoh was able to act wisely. A dreamer and the son of a dreamer, Joseph knew that God speaks through dreams and visions to save our lives and give us a future and a hope (Genesis 41:1-36).

Following the death of his grandmother, Stephen had a dream in which he heard his grandmother's voice and smelled the perfume she regularly wore. He felt her deep love for him and received a sense that he would find answers to the challenges he was facing. When he awakened, he felt a breeze blow through the room even though the windows were closed. Buoyed by his grandmother's presence, he felt new confidence that God was with him and would guide him on his personal and professional journey. He chose to become more attentive to God's vision for his life by dedicating himself to daily prayer and meditation and devotional reading. Stephen wonders if his grandmother was using this dream to point in the right direction. If love endures forever, then God may invite beloved relatives and friends to reach out to us from beyond the grave. The Celtic vision of "thin places" reminds us that heaven and earth permeate one another and that every place and encounter can reveal God's presence and wisdom for us. Love never ends and the energy of love that shapes us in this lifetime can still shape our paths. The deceased may reach out to us, piercing the veil of life and death, with guidance for our personal journeys. In the intricate interconnectedness of life, we may also call upon the saints, whether mystics of an earlier era or the "saints" of our own lives, to give us guidance and sustain and protect us in times of trial and temptation.

A DEEPER KNOWING

We are all connected with God and one another. The Grace of Interdependence, the fundamental goodness of life, which undergirds our freedom and creativity, even when these go astray, is grounded in God's Wisdom moving in and through all things. Within the Biblical tradition, this wisdom was reflected in the prophetic tradition and the ministry of Jesus and the early church. Inspired by God, persons experienced and participated in bringing forth "signs and wonders" in partnership with the abundantly-creative and loving Triune God.

Inspired by God's creative and challenging word, the Hebraic prophets warned the national leaders about the consequences of their actions. In their mystical experiences inspired by their relationship with the God of Israel and All Creation, prophets appeared to predict the future. While they may not have had paranormal experiences themselves, they were given insight into the moral nature of the universe. God spoke to them in dreams, visions, and words and they were able to glimpse from their finite perspective the Heart and Mind of God. These warnings had the character of premonitions or predictions about the future. They saw clearly that injustice, immorality, and idolatry would lead to national destruction. They lamented that neglect of the vulnerable persons would lead to a famine of hearing God's word despite elaborate worship services and generous offerings to the Temple.

Often the prophetic experience was described in terms of a "word of God" coming to a particular person. These words of God were personal and communal addresses, revealing to the prophet God's heart and vision for their nation's leaders and the world. Commitment to God's Shalom leads to national well-being and joy and laughter in the countryside and city streets. Turning away from God's vision of Shalom leads to polarization, economic disruption, and national destruction. The prophets did not predict the future in specifics, but experienced empathetically the interdependence of life and God's own passion for justice. The prophetic experience of Divine Pathos, God's empathetic passion for justice and God's sensitivity, inspired the prophetic critique of Israel and Judah.[1]

The prophets "predicted" the probable destruction of the nation and, beyond the day of reckoning, the hope of salvation that lies beyond destruction. Although they did not know the timetable of the coming Messiah, their experience of God's vision enabled them to live in hope of a Savior for Israel and humankind, the One Christians call, Jesus the Christ. In the same manner, John's visions on the Isle of Patmos were not predictive, but fathomed the depths of human experience and the intricacies of history. The two thousand year attempt to discern "the signs of the times" is doomed to failure, since John's intention was guidance and not prediction. Like his prophetic predecessors, John envisioned an alternative future to Roman persecution and religious half-heartedness, in which God would triumph over evil and humankind and nature would be restored to wholeness. The prophet assured that for those who remained faithful to God's wisdom in Jesus Christ, grace would abound and they would be victorious, despite threats to life and limb. Then and now, prophets can intuitively, imaginatively, and empathetically discern the "signs of the times" and God's responses to humankind's economic, social, and political values.

Most intuitive knowing, whether clairvoyant or telepathic, tends to be less political in nature than the prophetic admonitions or John's mystical vision. Still persons claim to have premonitions, or information about future events. On the global scale, persons report visions of planes crashing into skyscrapers, and then are astonished when such events, such as the terrorist attacks on 9/11, occur. On a personal scale, individuals often have dreams about apparently future events, involving themselves or others. Abraham Lincoln is said to have dreamed about his body lying in state just few weeks before his own assassination. Others, like my father-in-law, dream of disasters and warn loved ones to change their course

---

1   My understanding of the prophets is shaped by Abraham Joshua Heschel's *The Prophets: Two Volumes* (Peabody: MA, 2014) and Walter Brueggemann's *Prophetic Imagination* (Minneapolis: Fortess Press, 2014).

of action. Still others have an inclination to stay home only to discover paying attention to that still, small voice saved their lives from a terrorist attack, plane crash, or a natural disaster.

Sometimes missing choir practice can save your life. On a winter's day in 1950, Pastor Walter Klempel went to church early to light the furnace at Westside Baptist Church in Beatrice, Nebraska, in preparation for the evening's choir practice. As a rule, the fifteen choir members arrived on time for practice. But, this night, no one came to the 7:20 p.m. practice. At 7:25 p.m., the furnace blew up, destroying the building, and damaging several homes in the neighborhood. Anyone in the building at the time would have been killed, but that night the church was empty, leading people to ask "How could the whole choir have chosen to be absent on the same night?" As a pastor, who convenes study groups on a regular basis, I am well aware that attendance can vacillate from week to week, but someone, especially the teacher or choir director, always shows up! Experts calculated that there was less than a one in a million chance that everyone would stay home. But, to the person, some rather unimportant event — waiting for daughters to get dressed, getting involved in homework, stopping to see parents, or simply feeling tired — kept them away. Could there have been a Deeper Wisdom at work, "barring the door," so to speak to insure the safety of the choir members? Might such wisdom always be inspiring us, guiding our steps, and inviting us to listen and respond, either consciously or unconsciously? Physician Larry Dossey believes this event "illustrates the subtlety of premonitions — how they often manifest so faintly in our unconscious mind that we respond to them without knowing it. Conscious premonitions may make better headlines, but it is in the delicate, faint traces of awareness that future knowing most commonly presents itself."[1]

Such experiences invite us to consider whether we are children of divine predestination or creative participants in an open-ended adventure. Is everything connected in an Eternal Now, in which

---

1 Larry Dossey, *The Science of Premonitions* (New York: Penguin, 2010), 44. For the detailed account, see 41-44.

past, present, and future are joined in God's knowledge of yester-
day, today, and tomorrow; or in some form of predestation? Or,
is the universe so intricately connected that we can catch glimpses
of the future in its novelty? These glimpses, as theologian David
Griffin asserts, are probabilities and not actualities until they have
occurred. In experiencing the connection of past, present, and future, we can experience the textures of tomorrow even though they
have not actually occurred or cannot fully be known by us at the
time. Most premonitions are not precise but ambient. We see an
impression, intuit an outcome, or image a possibility, and then discover the congruence of our experience with what actually occurs.
Could it be that the pathway to the future is always found in the
present and that especially intuitive minds can chart broadly what
may occur in the unfolding of history?

Certain persons have the ability to intuit the emotional and
spiritual lives of others. Through non-sensory experiences, medical intuitives or empaths, some of whom believe they are guided
by spiritual beings, are able to assess the source of emotional or
physical ailments. According to this approach, medical intuitives
such as Carolyn Myss or Edgar Cayce, are able to tap into another's
emotional and physical life clairvoyantly. A medical intuitive whose
gifts I respect notes that she simply makes a spiritual connection
which allows her to experience what's going at the spiritual dimensions of her patients' lives. She believes that these spiritual or auric
dimensions are manifested in the quality of our physical well-being,
and that they can intuit the spiritual origins of illness long before
physical symptoms occur.

Are such experiences of empathy, healing dreams, premonitions, or deep connectedness, paranormal, and restricted to a few
people with special sensitivities or gifts, or are they, as physician
Larry Dossey affirms, reflections a deeper reality available to all
of us but seldom experienced because we do not cultivate psychic, mystical, or intuitive experiences? If, as Dossey and today's
process theologians assert, consciousness is grounded in a sea of
interconnected unconscious or superconscious experiences, then

such experiences are not miraculous, supernatural, or paranormal but reflect the impact of other dimensions of reality, shaping our lives apart from our typical awareness. Dreams, inspirations, intuitions, and guidance may be constantly at work in our lives, despite the fact we are only occasionally aware of them. If God is present everywhere seeking abundant life or all creation, then God is whispering to each of us in sighs too deep for words, in the unconscious and through synchronous encounters, and only occasionally do we consciously experience God's wisdom and vision for us and those persons and institutions we love. In the words of a slogan from the United Church of Christ, "God is still speaking." This divine voice comes in the call of tomorrow to embody justice and Shalom; it may also come in insights that connect today with future possibilities. But, is anyone listening to God's gentle nudges and insights in the course of everyday life? When we listen, we become part of a greater mystery and synchronous and inspirational guidance and grace fill our days.

THEOLOGICAL REFLECTIONS ON MYSTERY

The Biblical tradition proclaims that the whole earth is full of God's glory (Isaiah 6:1-8) and that in God, we live and move and have our being (Acts 17:28). The Gospel of Thomas challenges us to cleave the wood and discover God's presence in nature and the human experience (Thomas, 77). An omnipresent God touches each moment and each life. A loving God caresses us with well-being and wisdom in the context of the details of our day to day lives. There is an "original wholeness," as Thomas Merton noted, that is at the depths of every moments' experience. Physician Larry Dossey writes of the universe in terms of One, Interconnected and Dynamic Mind. Along with many contemporary physicists, Dossey believes that some form of consciousness is at the heart of the universe. Experience is global and not restricted to humankind or to the intellect.

For Christians, that One Mind is God, who is also the Heart and Wisdom of the Universe. Going beyond pantheism, the belief that God and the world are one reality, the Biblical tradition, interpreted through the lens of process theology, sees all things in God and God in all things. In the call and response of the God and the world, whole and part, we are constantly receiving guidance congruent with our particular time and place. When we awaken to that guidance, we become attuned with God's vision. In such moments, healings occur and coincidences happen. Perhaps, they've been there all along, but finally, like Moses walking by the burning bush to tend his father-in-law's flocks, we notice it. Other insights and psychic intuitions come without notice or preparation. Perhaps for a moment we find ourselves in a spiritual "thin place," in which we can experience the world in greater vividness from a God's eye view. God is not a neutral or homogenous energy. The God who shows up in everyone's life, every moment of the day, may appear more fully in some lives and some moments of our own lives to convey important information or guidance for us and those around us. This doesn't diminish our freedom or the openness of the future. We can always say "no" to God, but even our turning away from divine inspiration leaves its subtle mark in the direction of our lives.

Within the Grace of Interdependence, we can experience the words and emotions of those beside us as well as those faraway. The reality of a collective unconscious or quantum entanglement reminds us that we are never alone and are always being touched by forces that are supportive of us, as well as neutral and negative events. The dynamic interdependence of life, combined with our particular emotional and intellectual sensitivities of life, makes possible experiencing another's feelings or shaping their lives through our prayers, regardless of the distance. As Larry Dossey, contemporary physicists, and process theologians aver, Mind or Spirit is non-local and omnipresent. Spirits in the world connects all of us, and sometimes we notice it. We may call such experiences "paranormal," but they like the power of prayer and healing touch, represent a "deeper normal," the positive presence of divinity, moving through the freedom, creativity, limitations, and even waywardness of creation in its wondrous and amazing, and sometimes conflicting, diversity.

SPIRITUAL PRACTICE: CALLING ON THE SPIRIT

PRAYING WITH YOUR SPIRIT OPEN

British theologian and pastor, William Temple, proclaimed that "when I pray, coincidences happen, and when I don't, they don't." Temple's affirmation could be the underlying theme of this book. Experiences of angels, synchronicity, divine protection and inspiration, intuitive wisdom, and healing dreams are not anomalous nor are they supernatural, but reflect God's Wisdom and Providence moving through our intricately and dynamically connected world. God's presence is universal. God is the reality in whom we live, and move, and have our being. But, most of the time, we are oblivious to divine providence in its many forms, inspiration, intuition, guidance, protection, and coincidence. Grace abounds but we also need to "work out our salvation with fear and trembling," or awe and energy, to more fully experience the gifts God has in store for us (Philippians 2:12). To be more aware of divine guidance, simply keep your eyes open. Ask God to give you a deeper vision into everyday life and provide you with the insights you need to be one of God's companions in healing the world.

PRAYING FOR GUIDANCE AND CRYING FOR A VISION

A remarkable story from the early Christian movement provides guidance as to how we as persons and members of congregations might open to God's Wisdom more fully, based on the premise that God wants us and our congregations and communities to have abundant life and that God provides opportunities moment by moment for us to discern how best to be agents of healing

and abundance. Following the death of Judas, there was need for
a twelfth apostle to spread the good news of Jesus. Not exactly
knowing who might be best, the disciples turned to the primary
spiritual discipline they had learned from the Teacher and Healer:

> *So one of the men who have accompanied us during all the
> time that the Lord Jesus went in and out among us, beginning
> from the baptism of John until the day when he was taken up
> from us—one of these must become a witness with us to his resur-
> rection." So they proposed two, Joseph called Barsabbas, who was
> also known as Justus, and Matthias. Then they prayed and said,
> "Lord, you know everyone's heart. Show us which one of these two
> you have chosen to take the place in this ministry and apostleship
> from which Judas turned aside to go to his own place." And they
> cast lots for them, and the lot fell on Matthias; and he was added
> to the eleven apostles.*   – Acts 1:21-25

The women and men prayed! Then, they sought to discern the
best course of action.

They didn't act precipitously, but waited on God's timing and
the deeper rhythms of revelation that quietly guide our personal
and congregational paths. When the time was right, they called
for a decision, trusting the synchronicity of Divine Providence to
guide them to the right persons. While casting lots, choosing a particular stone or length of straw, might not be our congregation's or
our personal practice in making decisions, it is clear that the early
church believed God would give us signs, or guideposts, to point
us in the right direction. To paraphrase William Temple, when we
pray, inspirations come. When we ask for help, help is on the way.
Seek, ask, and knock. God's always acting in our lives, but in the
asking, seeking, and knocking we find the answers and pathways
we need at this moment in time. We create a field of energy, a
space for inspiration that enables God to be more present in our
decision-making. God wants us to be active rather than passive. The
Loving Parent provides guidance so that our actions are congruent
with what is best for us and others.

If you wish to have deeper wisdom and greater intuition for the good of the world, then pray. Ask for help and guidance. And, then listen. In deep listening, we may hear the still, small voice of God; we may tap into another's emotional life; we may more clearly experience God's vision; we may have dreams that provide greater wisdom than the conscious mind. Grace and wisdom are always coming to us, but we need to embrace the gifts of God for us and others. Intuitive and inspirational experiences are not just for individual gain but for the well-being of the whole, our church, community, and the planet.

This process of asking for God's vision, crying out for a vision, as the First Americans say, is the work of communities as well as individuals. What would happen in your congregation if everyone prayed for God's vision for the church? What if the church was a laboratory for visionary, synchronous, and intuitive experiences? What if we shared our deepest intuitions for mission and program, and then placed our visions, without ego attachment, in the hands of the congregation? We can only imagine what the result might be in terms of spiritual growth and congregational mission. In the spirit of the early Christian movement, I believe new ideas would emerge, dead ends would be opened up, and lively energies fall upon the church. Every day would have the feel of Pentecost!

So simply, ask for guidance, and pause long enough to quietly listen for God's sighs moving within you; sighs that are too deep for words in their disclosure of the Heart of God.

CHAPTER FIVE

IN SEARCH OF THE MIRACULOUS

Now there was a woman who had been suffering from hemorrhages for twelve years. She had endured much under many physicians, and had spent all that she had; and she was no better, but rather grew worse. She had heard about Jesus, and came up behind him in the crowd and touched his cloak, for she said, "If I but touch his clothes, I will be made well." Immediately her hemorrhage stopped; and she felt in her body that she was healed of her disease. Immediately aware that power had gone forth from him, Jesus turned about in the crowd and said, "Who touched my clothes?" And his disciples said to him, "You see the crowd pressing in on you; how can you say, 'Who touched me?'" He looked all around to see who had done it. But the woman, knowing what had happened to her, came in fear and trembling, fell down before

him, and told him the whole truth. He said to her, "Daughter,
your faith has made you well; go in peace, and be healed of your
disease."   – Mark 5:25-34

Forty years ago, my father was diagnosed with his second hernia. At the time, hernia operations were invasive and often involved
a recovery period of several weeks before the patient could return to
normal everyday activities. My father had been through that before
and didn't want the ordeal of a second operation. In great pain, my
father, to use the language of my childhood Baptist faith, "took it
to the Lord in prayer." In a few days, his symptoms disappeared,
never to return again in the next thirty years of his life. My father
was sure that God answered his prayers. He knew he'd experienced
a miracle, a surprising act of God that turned his life around.

Paul affirms: "I should be dead, but God healed me through
prayer. Until I was diagnosed with untreatable cancer, I didn't take
my prayer life seriously. I still wasn't sure that prayer made a difference, but I took a chance. I had nothing to lose, so I put my
life in God's hands. I read the healing stories from the Bible, and
began to believe that God could change my life. I was desperate
and had no other choice, given my medical prognosis of incurable
cancer. Our congregation had a weekly healing service, and on the
spur of the moment, I decided to go. It was a simple service. No
fanfare or bombast: just scripture, prayer, and anointing with oil.
Nothing dramatic happened but I went home feeling at peace, and
thanked God for his healing touch. A few weeks later, I returned
to the hospital for a C-T scan and bloodwork, and to everyone's
surprise, the cancer was gone. That was seven years ago, and I'm
still cancer free. I still go the doctor for regular checkups. I don't
know exactly what happened. But, I believe that God answered my
prayers and because of the prayers of my friends and that simple
healing service, I was cured." Steve confesses that he doesn't know
how this healing occurred, nor even when it occurred. He knows
about "spontaneous remissions" and is committed to receiving the
best medical care to keep his blood pressure in check. He also

believes that he experienced a miracle. "God was there, that's all I know, and today I'm alive."

I grew up listening Kathryn Kuhlman softly whispering, "I believe in miracles." I saw Oral Roberts slapping persons on the forehead and shouting, "Be healed." My parents were praying people and every time I opened the refrigerator door, I was confronted by a plastic magnet that pronounced, "Prayer changes things." I grew up hearing testimonies of divine intervention to cure serious illnesses, heal marriages, and deliver people from addictions. No one could explain them, but it was clear to our faith community that God's miraculous power was at work to heal the sick and bless our lives. We couldn't discern why some people weren't cured, despite our fervent prayers. We used language to describe the mysteries of life and death with phrases like "God had a reason" or "it wasn't God's will" or "God has a plan and it's not our place to question." The televangelists claimed spontaneous healings from the hand of God. Sometimes, to my chagrin, they also appeared to blame those who didn't get well with explanations like "They didn't have enough faith" or "Maybe there was a sin they didn't confess."

Over the years, I've encountered many people who believe that they were cured as a result of the power of prayer and faith in the healing Christ. I have also heard testimonies of spontaneous remissions among everyday people who simply went on with their lives, without praying for healings or requesting the prayers of others. They rejoiced at their good fortune, but remained agnostic about the cause. "I was one in a million. Just my dumb luck," as one friend explained. Whether or not God is invoked, the word "miracle" is evoked to describe mysterious deliverance from incurable and chronic illnesses of mind, body, and spirit.

IN SEARCH OF THE MIRACULOUS

The Bible is a guidebook on miraculous living. God provides a way where there is no way. The Holy One parts the seas, calms the storms, liberates captives, heals the sick, and defeats the powers of darkness and death. Long before church theologians and philosophers paused heaven and earth, spirit and flesh, mind and body, and individual and community, the Biblical tradition affirmed that God was at work in every event. God was in this place, Jacob stammered, after his dream of a ladder of angels. In Christ, the Word became flesh and dwelled among us. God's healing light shines in and through everyone. God is the reality in whom we live and move and have our being. The whole world, according to these Biblical mystics, reflects an intimate and passionate God for whom, as the prophets note, even the weights and measure of merchants are of spiritual consequence. God hears the cries of the poor and sends prophets with inspired calls to justice. God moves through the wind and the waves, the laughter of children, and the healing of the human heart. Deep down in this enchanted universe, in which everything that breathes praises God, all is miracle (Psalm 148, 150).

While many people see miracles as divine interventions from the outside, violating predicable laws of nature, the Biblical tradition sees God's Gentle Providence moving through all things. God is here right where we are and in every situation, and doesn't need to be imported from the outside or invoked by our prayers. God wants us to have abundant life (John 10:10). Miracles are everywhere. Synchronous encounters and burning bushes dot our paths. Healing dreams come with every night's sleep.

Still, we search for the miraculous. While miracles are not supernatural invasions from the outside, there are moments in which God's love and power bursts forth, not as an alien force, but as the deepest reality of the universe and our lives. God, who inspired the big bang and cast forth the galaxies, patiently guides our lives and gives us strength for the journey. I believe the miraculous is natural, and also exceptional. There are moments of power and transformation, moments in which our cells and souls are transformed. There are acts of power, energetic bursts, mystical experiences, in which the divine and human are united to bring healing and wholeness to our world. As I've noted throughout this book, the Celtic Christians called certain places "thin places," where heaven and earth meet, and our lives are illuminated. The Church father Iranaeus described the glory of God as a human being who is fully alive, and transparent to God's wisdom and healing energy. Could miraculous healings reflect the congruence of moments of unique divine presence and the openness of more fully alive humans?

Miracles reflect in superlative ways God's Gentle Providence. They are acts of grace, filled with meaning, that change the course of our lives. Sometimes they occur spontaneously without any preparation or faith on our part. Other times, in the dynamic call and response of God and the world, our prayers open us to God's loving energy and we — and those we love — are transformed. We become new creations and life triumphs over death.

There is no single, fully adequate definition of a miracle. Still, I believe that miracles reflect the intersection of God's Providence and human openness: acts of power, acts of love, acts of creative transformation, coming forth as quantum leaps to change our cells and souls from sickness to health, and death to life. These acts of power and transformation are personal, intimate, and concrete and reveal in our dynamic and interdependent world of space and time, God's vision of Shalom. They astound us. They change our hearts and cast out the powers of darkness. They remind us, as Walt Whitman proclaimed, that all is miracle, and each moment can elicit in our spirits what Abraham Joshua Heschel described as radical amazement.

SCIENCE IS STUDYING THE SACRED

The wall between science and scripture has, like the walls of Jericho, "Come tumbling down," opening a pathway to a new partnership between persons of faith and physicians and health-care givers. The disastrous dualism between mind and body, and spirituality and science, characteristic of the rise of the modern era has been challenged by medical researchers as well as spiritual guides and healers. The holistic vision of Jesus of Nazareth, along with ancient health care practices such as acupuncture, *qigong*, healing touch, and yoga, has been integrated with the latest medical technologies. Physicians as well as laypersons have discovered the necessity of both "high touch" and "high tech" for personal whole-ness and well-being. Major hospitals offer courses and employee professionals in the areas of mindfulness meditation, yoga for stress reduction, and reiki healing touch. As physician Dale Matthews as-serts, good healthcare involves both prayer and Prozac. Meditation as well as medication has been found to make a difference in pain relief, stress reduction, blood pressure, and recovery from illness.

Researchers are discovering that prayer is good medicine and that the faith factor promotes overall well-being. While still in its infancy stage, prayer or distant intentionality has been associated with enhanced recovery from surgery. Energy work, or prayer with your hands, has been found to make a positive difference in the growth of plants and the healing of wounds among mice. The faith factor suggests that our beliefs and attitudes can shape our well-be-ing as well as the well-being of other persons, not to mention plants and animals in our environments. The interdependence of the uni-verse, reflected in the intricate connectedness of mind, body, and spirit, opens the door for a new partnership among spiritual and medical healers. Jesus' affirmation "your faith has made you well" has been found to complement "better living through chemistry."[1]

Quantum entanglement, humorously described by Einstein as "spooky action at a distance," suggests that we are all connected and that paranormal experiences and whole person spiritual healing are essential aspects of human experiences. We live in a world of mysteries, miracles, and wonder.

---

1   See Larry Dossey, *Healing Words* (San Francisco: Harper One, 1995); Larry Dossey, *Prayer is Good Medicine* (San Francisco: Harper One, 1997); Harold Koenig, *The Healing Power of Faith* (New York: Simon and Schuster, 2001); Dale Matthews, *The Faith Factor: Proof of the Healing Power of Prayer* (New York: Penguin, 1999); Candace Pert, *The Molecules of Emotion: The Science Behind Mind-Body Medicine* (New York: Simon and Schuster, 1999).

Jesus the Healer

While many nineteenth and twentieth century theologians and ministers dismissed the healing ministry of Jesus as a vestige of a pre-scientific and mythical world view of interest only to Pentecostals and holy rollers, Jesus has been rediscovered as a healer in mainstream and progressive congregations. No longer an embarrassment to educated people and to liberal Christians, Jesus has been embraced as a truly holistic healer, who joined prayer, faith, and touch, with the medical practices of his time. Mainline and progressive congregations, like the one I pastor, have initiated healing services, prayer and meditation groups, sponsor yoga classes and reiki healing clinics, and explore the relationship of complementary medicine to the healing ministry of the church. Jesus' healing ministry reveals that God is concerned about bodies as well as spirits and earth as well heaven. Jesus' ministry awakened persons to the miraculous, to the reality of amazing of acts of power, and signs and wonders, that reveal the heart of God and God's vision of abundant life for all God's children. Jesus shows people then and now that God cares for us and that miracles occur in the lively interplay of God's loving energy and human faith. Not violations of God's dependable laws of nature, revealed in summer and winter and seedtime and harvest, Jesus' healings reflect God's great faithfulness and invite us to explore deeper levels of reality, in which our response to God's grace through prayer, faith, and personal support, can be factors in transforming cells as well as souls.[1]

In this section, we will explore Jesus' healing miracles, involving human life and the non-human world, to awaken our sense of the miraculous power of God to heal those who suffer from the

---

1   See Bruce Epperly, *God's Touch: Faith, Wholeness, and the Healing Miracles of Jesus* (Louisville: Westminster/John Knox, 2002; *Healing Marks: Healing and Spirituality in Mark's Gospel* (Energion Publications, 2012); *Healing Worship: Purpose and Practice* (Cleveland: Pilgrim Press, 2006); Morton Kelsey, *Healing and Christianity* (Minneapolis: Fortress Press, 1995); Tilda Norberg and Robert Webber, *Stretch Out Your Hand: Exploring Healing Prayer* (Upper Room, Nashville, 1998).

brokenness of mind, body, spirit, and relationships. I began this chapter with the story of a woman with a flow of blood. The victim of a chronic illness that made each day a misery and also caused her to be viewed as an outcast, moral inferior, and threat by her neighbors, she comes to Jesus as her last hope. She is afraid to touch his body, for fear of contaminating him. Her soul cries out for healing, if she only can get the chance to touch his clothes. When she touches Jesus, a power (Greek: *dunamis*) goes out from him. The Greek word suggests an inherent energy or strength, which comes from within. It is divine power, but it is also the power of the universe, the power of big bang, of energy or chi coursing through our bodies, that can be brought forth in the confluence of our faith and God's Wise Energy. This is a miracle of transformation, emerging from the heart of reality, the Wisdom or the Word (John 1:1-5, 9) that created and guides the universe and is the spiritual core of each creature. When we have the right convergence of faith, prayer, the faith of others, a healing environment, and God's prevenient aim at abundant life, miracles occur and life transforming power is released. Persons experience miracles from God's Nature and not an alien unearthly force.

The corresponding story, that of Jairus' daughter, affirms that miracles — releases of healing energy — occur when God's loving power is met by human faith. Jesus tosses out the naysayers and creates a healing circle, a little church dedicated to this girl's well-being. Jesus' own optimism, seeing her as asleep and not dead, awakens the community to a higher energy, the energy of love, that moves mountains, makes a way where there is no way, and can change the very structure of our cells (Mark 5:21-24, 35-43; Luke 8:41-42, 49-56).

We are often impatient with prayer. We want the solutions to our problems immediately. Sometimes, however, it takes a while for the medicine to kick in or the bone to heal. In the same way, the healing of mind, body, and spirit may be "telescoped" in dramatic ways, but most of the time healing is deliberate and requires us to be patient with God's healing energies and our prayers and the prayers of others working with our lives. Mark 8:22-26 is one of my favorite healing miracles. I feel an affinity with the sight impaired man. The healings that I have experienced and prayed for with others have typically taken a long time, and sometimes there have been physical and spiritual relapses. Yet, God persists and because God hasn't given up on my life, I find the courage to accept my imperfection and failure with hope that God is at work, guiding me by God's healing vision.

> *They came to Bethsaida. Some people brought a blind man to him and begged him to touch him. He took the blind man by the hand and led him out of the village; and when he had put saliva on his eyes and laid his hands on him, he asked him, "Can you see anything?" And the man looked up and said, "I can see people, but they look like trees, walking." Then Jesus laid his hands on his eyes again; and he looked intently and his sight was restored, and he saw everything clearly. Then he sent him away to his home, saying, "Do not even go into the village."* – Mark 8:22-26

In life, we not only are challenged to "*expect* a miracle," but also to "*accept* a miracle." Recently, I had an inspiration as I was receiving a quantum healing treatment. I heard an inner voice, whispering "accept the healing that you need." It gave no timetable, nor did it specify the healing that I needed. This insight alerted me to be on the lookout for God's healing in its many forms. We never fully know ourselves, nor the healings we need; we have to trust the timing and the healing to God's ever-present and ever-active grace.

At first glance, Jesus and the sight-impaired man appear to fail in their quest for healing. Still, Jesus does not give up, nor does he blame the sigh-impaired man for a deficiency in faith. Jesus simply goes back to work, healing the man gradually through a combination of prayer, touch, and folk medicine. Miracles can emerge though medication and meditation and Prozac and prayer. "Miracle drugs" are simply that; expression of divine wisdom and healing touch in pharmaceutical form. The Great Physician moves through cells and souls. The Healer from Nazareth transforms our lives through energetic healing touch, laying on of hands, anointing with oil, visualization, and spoken and meditative prayer along with the latest medical and pharmaceutical advances. God is fully present in our world and works through a variety of holistic and technological healing media to bring forth quantum leaps of life-transforming energy, moving through and with and not contrary with natural healing processes.

Today, readers of the Bible may be able to accept Jesus' healings in light of whole person and complementary medicine, and as reflections of the placebo effect and faith factor. Our attitudes have physical correlates. Positive affirmations can be life-giving, energizing our spirits and lifting up our bodies. Positive visualizations can be factors in pain relief, recovery from illness, reduction of symptoms, and deepening of our spiritual lives. A change in mind can register as a change in physiology. Optimism can open the door to an influx of divine energy. Faith can be the tipping point between health and illness. What is more challenging to contemporary readers are the nature miracles, including Moses' parting the waters, Jesus walking on water, and Jesus calming a storm at sea.

> On that day, when evening had come, he said to them, "Let us go across to the other side." And leaving the crowd behind, they took him with them in the boat, just as he was. Other boats were with him. A great windstorm arose, and the waves beat into the boat, so that the boat was already being swamped. But he was in the stern, asleep on the cushion; and they woke him up and said to him, "Teacher, do you not care that we are perishing?" He woke up and rebuked the wind, and said to the sea, "Peace! Be still!" Then the wind ceased, and there was a dead calm. He said to them, "Why are you afraid? Have you still no faith?" And they were filled with great awe and said to one another, "Who then is this, that even the wind and the sea obey him?"
>
> – Mark 4:35-41

Can our prayers and spiritual practices shape the non-human world around us?

Throughout history, rainmakers and shamans have claimed a transformative congruence between spirituality and changes in the weather. By using chants and spiritual formulae, these spiritual leaders believed they could coax rain from the clouds and shape weather patterns. Jesus also appeared to have power over nature. At first glance such power in relationship to nature appears an unbelievable vestige of an archaic world view. However, in a dynamic, interdependent universe, within which God seeks abundant life for all creation, a divine-human partnership is possible that can influence weather patterns. Moreover, if, as the Psalmist says, all things can praise God (Psalm 148 and 150), then we truly live in an "enchanted universe." Some degree of relationship and experience is universal, including in the non-human and microscopic worlds. God can enter the experience of human beings, and also move in the forces of nature. Accordingly, in an interdependent enchanted universe, we can influence from the inside as well as externally non-human life just as our prayers influence other humans.

Many of us have heard about the Butterfly Effect, describing the impact small changes in shaping large-scale happenings. In the poetry of the Butterfly Effect, whose origins were in a meteorological lab in Cambridge, Massachusetts, it is believed that a butterfly flapping her wings in Monterey, California, given a lapse of a few weeks, can be a factor in a thunderstorm on Cape Cod. Weather patterns reflect dynamic and fluid relationships, each of which may involve a variety of factors, not the least of which is our intentionality.

In a similar fashion, Canadian psychologist Bernard Grad studied distant or non-local causation (psychokinesis) with energy healer Oscar Estebany. Using energy healing techniques, Estebany was able to promote healing in mice and increase the growth of barley seeds that were given water that had been placed in a bottle Estebany held between his hands. Given the nature of the subjects, seeds and rice, we can rule out the placebo effect or hypnosis as factors in the difference between the control group and Estebany's subjects.[1]

---

1 David Ray Griffin, *Parapsychology, Spirituality, and Spirituality: A Postmodern Exploration* (Albany: State University of New York Press, 1997), 87-88/

In a similar fashion, Presbyterian minister and scientist Franklin Loehr studied the power of prayer on plants. Those plants directly prayed for germinated faster than plants in the control group which were not the object of the participants' prayers. Praying for the water used in the germination process also produced greater flora growth. In contrast, plants that were "cursed," the objects of negative prayer, grew more slowly or stopped growing entirely.[1]

Given the possibility that our spiritual state can influence the natural world, is it possible that Jesus' prayers could have stilled the storm? Did his spiritual power somehow calm the waves? Was his relationship with God so strong that even the winds and waves obeyed him? In the dynamic and enchanted universe described by scripture and quantum physics, in particular quantum entanglement theory, which suggests that two particles can influence one another despite vast geographical distances, we can imagine that such events are possible. Can the intentionality of a highly evolved spiritual being influence natural events to support human well-being? The possibility of such events invites us to embrace a world of mysteries and miracles!

A THEOLOGY OF MIRACLES

In his book on premonitions, Larry Dossey expresses his discomfort with using the words "paranormal" and "parapsychology," because they create a false impression that experiences of psychic connection, joining past, present, and what we perceive to be future events are abnormal or unnatural. Dossey asserts that psychic phenomena "are part of a part of nature, and not *para,* or apart."[2] I feel the same way about the use of the word "miracle" to describe life-transforming bursts of energy and inspiration that reverse diseases of mind, body, and spirit. I believe our faith can

---

1   Franklin Loehr, *The Power of Prayer on Plants* (New York: Signet, 1969). See also http://quantum-agri-phils.com/PowerofPrayeronSeedsandPlants. pdf

2   Larry Dossey, *The Science of Premonitions,* xv.

move mountains and that faith can change physical well-being in amazing ways. I also believe that faith wells up from within us in relationship to God's Gentle and sometimes Dramatic Providence. Inherent in nature and in our physical bodies is the possibility of unexpected and transformative reversals of health and changes in weather patterns. These are "miracles" because these events transform our lives in radical ways. We seem to be beneficiaries of actions of powers greater and wiser than ourselves. Further, I hesitate to use the word "miracle" as the result of its identification by some theologians and preachers with divine supernatural activity, breaking into the otherwise uninspired and insentient secular world, as well with the shenanigans of certain televangelists. I believe that God is the personal and loving energy within which we live and move and have our being. We don't have to beg for God's concern for us; God already loves us and wants what's best for us, congruent with our life-situation and the well-being of others. We don't have to import God into our world as some sort of illegal or undocumented alien; God is already here, moving through our lives, our cells, thoughts, and external circumstances. Prayer and healing touch make a difference but they are reflections of God's love moving in our lives and not the invocation of an otherwise indifferent deity.

Our world is miraculous without needing miracles from the outside. In the interplay of human openness and divine love, we can have miracles without supernaturalism. We are more wonderful and powerful than we can imagine and so is God. We are, as Gandhi affirms, the change we have been looking for. God is "still speaking," as the United Church of Christ affirmation states, and God is ready to give us more than we can ask or imagine.

A theology of miracles begins and ends with God, especially as we understand God through the life, teachings, and healing ministry of Jesus of Nazareth, our Savior and Healer, and the One who reveals the power and character of God to us. Speaking for God, Jesus proclaims that God wants us to flourish in every way. Jesus came that we might have life in all its abundance (John 10:10).

Jesus also wants everyone to flourish, as he proclaims in his first public message:

> *"The Spirit of the Lord is upon me,*
> *because he has anointed me*
> *to bring good news to the poor.*
> *He has sent me to proclaim release to the captives*
> *and recovery of sight to the blind,*
> *to let the oppressed go free,*
> *to proclaim the year of the Lord's favor."*
> — Luke 4:18-19

A theology of miracles begins with the affirmation that God loves the world (John 3:16) and desires that all creation experience Shalom, God's wholeness, peace, and well-being. Sickness, division, polarization, and evil abound; but this is not God's will, nor does God directly cause war, pestilence, or sickness. God does not send a tsunami, hurricanes, or AIDS to punish wayward humankind. God does not soften our nation's defenses to permit terrorist attacks, as some televangelists have suggested. God does not cause cancer, heart disease, ALS, or Alzheimer's. As Jesus says, "for [God] makes his sun rise on the evil and on the good, and sends rain on the righteous and on the unrighteous" (Matthew 5:45). God is love and God's love is the healing counterforce, transforming and eventually saving all of us, including the forces of evil.

A theology of miracles expects great things of God and of us. Divine energy is everywhere. God is alive and moving in our world. God is neither impotent nor omnipotent. God works within the world as it is, the world God creates and guides, toward a vision of what the world can be. In every moment, God presents the world, and each part of it, with possibilities for growth, healing, and reconciliation. These are not abstract possibilities, coming from the outside. They are personal and relevant to who we are and our greatest dreams and weaknesses. God has a personal relationship with all creation, and this personal relationship is worked out, like all personal relationships, in the context of our freedom and creativity. God is in this place right where we are and right where our loved ones are. God wants us and our loved ones to be healed. But, we can be oblivious to God's call and choose the ways of death rather than life. When we open ourselves to God's healing touch, God is able to do greater things and encourages us to do greater things than we can imagine. God wants us to be adventurous agents in transforming our own lives and the world in which we live. In speaking of God's presence in the world, Agnes Sanford who revived healing ministries within the Episcopalian church proclaims:

> God is within us and without us. He is the source of all life; and of unimaginable depths of inter-stellar space. But he is also the indwelling life of our own little selves.   And just as the whole world of electricity will not light a house unless the house itself is prepared to receive that electricity, so the infinite and eternal God cannot help us unless we are prepared to receive that light within ourselves.[1]

The world in which we live is profoundly dynamic and interdependent. The world is constantly changing and this opens the door to healing possibilities. The universe is not stuck in the past, but moving toward the future. The concrete world, including our personal and community past, is the womb of possibility. The past and our environmental context condition the landscape of possibility, enabling us to experience likely possibilities as premonitions. This same landscape of possibility contains all we need to be whole, whether or not we or those we love receive the cure we seek. The ultimate healing is a relationship with God, and when there cannot be a cure, there can always be a healing as a result of God's tender care and God's invitation to everlasting life in companionship with Jesus our Healer and Savior.

In the profound interdependence of life, some moments are truly miraculous. Spirits are transformed, addictions cured, and cells rejuvenated. These moments are not unnatural or supernat-

---

1   Agnes Sanford, *The Healing Light* (St. Paul: Macalester Park Publishing, 1972), 19.

ural but our deepest legacy in a God-filled universe. When there is an alignment of God's vision, human openness, the prayers of others, healing environments, and synchronous events, leaps in energy occur. Sometimes these bursts of transforming energy may even occur when we are unaware of it. God works just as fully in the unconscious, the realm of "sighs too deep for words," as in our conscious intentionality (Romans 8:26). It is true that our openness shapes the landscape of divine healing energy. However, like ourselves, God can — and does — choose to be more present in some moments than others as a reflection of God's vision of Shalom. When scripture says "God was in Christ reconciling the world (2 Corinthians 5:19)," it means that God who is present everywhere and in all things, chose — and still chooses — to be fully present, given our history as a race, in the person Jesus as a pathway to our own healing and wholeness. God always seeks our wholeness, but some moments may be more reflective of God's vision than others. In these moments, amazing energies and insights are released for our well-being and the healing of our world.

John's Gospel proclaims, the true light of God shines on everyone (John 1:10). Still, that ubiquitous healing light may shine more brightly when there is a confluence of God's will and our openness. In those moments, we recognize and experience something miraculous that takes us from fear to love, sickness to health, and death to life. Ultimately this happens on God's terms and timetable and not our own.

In my first book on health and spirituality, written over twenty years ago, I told the story of a young boy's prayers. Whenever he lost a ball in his backyard, he asked God to help him find it. Sometimes, he even challenged God to give him a miracle of recovery. Many times, the lost ball was recovered and he gave thanks in his childlike way. More often, he could not recover the wayward spheres. Years later, that same boy, a grownup with a son of his own, returned to his parents' home. His father, now a widower, was unable to paint the house due to effects of the aging process, so the son volunteered to help out. As father and son trimmed bushes and cleared around the foundation, the boy's prayers were answered. He found more than a dozen lost balls. The balls were worse for wear, but the little boy's prayers were answered. This time his prayers were answered, not out of self-interest, but because he was helping his father. That boy was me. I am still learning to place my life, joy and sorrow, celebration and pain, grace and sin, in God's hands and trust that God is with me, that I am with God's grace in the change that I seek, and that each day God is giving me miracles beyond what I can ask or imagine.[1] Thanks be to the God of angels, mysteries, and miracles.

SPIRITUAL PRACTICE: CALLING THE GREAT PHYSICIAN

The great mystery of Christian faith is that Christ is alive and has promised that when we have faith in God, we can do greater things than we can imagine in bringing healing to ourselves and the world (John 14:12). God's healing light shines in all things. Beth-El, the gate of heaven, is everywhere, and God's healing energy is available to everyone who opens her or his heart and mind.

Jesus did not teach a methodology of healing. He used many techniques to elicit God's healing energy in the lives of those he encountered. Jesus still comes to us in a variety of healing paths. In Jesus' ministry, he transformed persons' lives, body, mind, spirit, and relationships, through practices such as healing touch, transfer of energy, transformational words, inspiring faith, creating healing circles, exorcizing evil spirits, prayer, distant healing, and integrating faith and medicine. Jesus was also aware that healers need to take time for personal refreshment and meditative prayer so that their own healing energy remains strong and focused. The following practices enable us to be more fully open to God's healing light and to experience God's miraculous grace in ways more than we ask or imagine.

---

1   I first told this story in *Spirituality and Health, Health and Spirituality* (Mystic, CT: Twenty-third Publications, 1997), 121-122.

LIVING IN THE LIGHT

John's Gospel proclaims that God's light shines in all human beings. In the words of the John's Prologue: "The true light, which enlightens everyone, was coming into the world" (John 1:9). Jesus tells his own disciples:

> *You are the light of the world. A city built on a hill cannot be hid. No one after lighting a lamp puts it under the bushel basket, but on the lampstand, and it gives light to all in the house. In the same way, let your light shine before others, so that they may see your good works and give glory to your Father in heaven.*
>
> – Matthew 5:14-16

God's healing light is everywhere, as Agnes Sanford proclaims. We just need to connect with it. In this exercise, take time to regularly sit in a comfortable position, breathing deeply and gently God's Spirit. Visualize that Spirit in terms of a healing light, filling your body from head to toe and illuminating your consciousness with every breath you take. Visualize God's healing energy going forth from you with every breath. God's energy flows in and through you toward everyone you meet. Let every encounter be an opportunity to bring healing to the world. Surround everyone you meet with a sense of God's healing light.

HEALING TOUCH

Jesus' ministry involved healing touch. Touch can transform our lives, connecting with God's power and bringing new energies into our lives. While it is helpful to learn various healing touch techniques such as reiki healing touch, therapeutic touch, healing touch, and quantum healing, all of which enhance and balance the energies that give life to mind, body, and spirit, simple prayerful touch can also mediate God's energy of love. Jesus laid hands on persons in need, bringing the fullness of grace into their lives. His touch changed their bodies, gave them new hope, welcomed them to God's new community, and empowered them to be God's companions in healing the world.

Touch heals when we call upon God, and are open to God's energy of love flowing through us. When you encounter persons in need, first quietly pray for their well-being. If healing touch is welcome, and you've asked permission, without fanfare place your hand on their forehead or another appropriate part of their body, praying for God's healing. For example, you may say, "In the name of Jesus, I pray that you experience healing in body, mind, and spirit. May you experience the fullness of God's blessing so that you will be, in your healing, an instrument for blessing others."

You may also use healing oils as a medium for God's healing touch. You may choose to anoint someone seeking God's healing touch by making the sign of the cross and praying for God to heal them fully and completely in body, mind, and spirit. Pray that they might experience the peace of Christ that surpasses all understanding.

HEALING CIRCLES

Jesus created a healing circle to restore Jairus' daughter to well-being. The faith of Jesus' companions and the girl's parents, like the faith of the woman with a chronic flow of blood, created a circle of love in which God's healing energies flowed without obstruction.

You can create healing circles either for yourself, a person in need of healing, or as a communal form of worship. In any case, the key element is to come together as a community of two or more in an affirmative spirit, trusting that God will fully supply our needs and the needs of those for whom we pray. Banish negativity as you open to healing affirmations, such as:

God's light shines in every cell of my [or her or his] body.

God will supply our every need.

God wants me [her or him] to have abundant life and we align ourselves with God's vision.

We are in God's circle of love and call upon God's Spirit to heal us in body, mind, and spirit.

As we touch hands, we are touching the hem of Jesus' garment. God's healing power flows through us, healing us in every way.

In the name of Jesus, we accept God's healing. We accept God's healing in the way that we need it today, trusting God with our future as well as our past.

A CONCLUDING WORD

We live in a world of mysteries and miracles. Angelic spirits touch our lives in challenging situations, liberating us from powers of darkness in ourselves and in our communities. We can never fully fathom the landscape of the spiritual world as it permeates and shapes everyday life. We can, however, turn toward the better angels in our daily lives, reach out for God's blessing and healing touch, and share that blessing with others. We can choose life when death is all around and love when others are motivated by fear and hate.

God's better angels are with us and invite us to become the change we want to see in the world. May your journey be filled with wonder and amazement, mystery and miracles, and may God's loving angels guide your path in companionship with Jesus, our Healer and Savior.

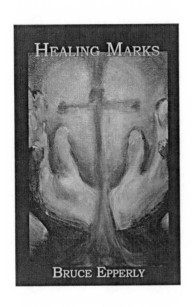
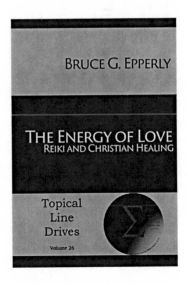

More from Energion Publications

Personal Study

Finding My Way in Christianity	Herold Weiss	$16.99
Holy Smoke! Unholy Fire	Bob McKibben	$14.99
The Jesus Paradigm	David Alan Black	$17.99
When People Speak for God	Henry Neufeld	$17.99
The Sacred Journey	Chris Surber	$11.99

Christian Living

Faith in the Public Square	Robert D. Cornwall	$16.99
Grief: Finding the Candle of Light	Jody Neufeld	$8.99
Crossing the Street	Robert LaRochelle	$16.99

Bible Study

Learning and Living Scripture	Lentz/Neufeld	$12.99
From Inspiration to Understanding	Edward W. H. Vick	$24.99
Luke: A Participatory Study Guide	Geoffrey Lentz	$8.99
Philippians: A Participatory Study Guide	Bruce Epperly	$9.99
Ephesians: A Participatory Study Guide	Robert D. Cornwall	$9.99

Theology

Creation in Scripture	Herold Weiss	$12.99
Creation: the Christian Doctrine	Edward W. H. Vick	$12.99
The Politics of Witness	Allan R. Bevere	$9.99
Ultimate Allegiance	Robert D. Cornwall	$9.99
History and Christian Faith	Edward W. H. Vick	$9.99
The Church Under the Cross	William Powell Tuck	$11.99
The Journey to the Undiscovered Country	William Powell Tuck	$9.99
Eschatology: A Participatory Study Guide	Edward W. H. Vick	$9.99

Ministry

Clergy Table Talk	Kent Ira Groff	$9.99
Out of the Office	Robert D. Cornwall	$9.99

Generous Quantity Discounts Available
Dealer Inquiries Welcome
Energion Publications — P.O. Box 841
Gonzalez, FL_ 32560
Website: http://energionpubs.com
Phone: (850) 525-3916

CPSIA information can be obtained
at www.ICGtesting.com
Printed in the USA
FFOW03n2000220917
40164FF